ADVANCE PRAISE

"People are an organization's most important source of competitive advantage and feedback is the key to unleashing their full potential. *FairTalk* offers leaders straight talk on how to open up communication on their teams, improving not only individual performance but creating a culture where feedback is an essential building block for success."

Ellyn Shook, chief leadership and
human resources officer, Accenture

"As business challenges require ever more creative, adaptive and collaborative organizations, leadership effectiveness has become mission-critical. Actionable feedback is one of the most impactful levers leaders have to build a smarter, more agile workforce. Angela Lane and Sergey Gorbatov have brought together science, real examples and a step-by-step process for giving fair, focused and credible feedback. *FairTalk* meets you as a leader where you are, allowing you to execute skilfully on the fundamental job of leadership: to maximize human potential."

Michael Chavez, CEO, Duke Corporate Education

"Prompt and pertinent feedback is essential for building employee engagement. This briskly written and entertaining book provides a set of sensible and systematic guidelines for structuring the feedback process."

Robert Hogan, PhD, president,
Hogan Assessment Systems

"*FairTalk* does a masterful job of synthesizing great research and advice, refracted through common sense to offer managers a really useful, practical guide to giving feedback in this world of triggers, snowflakes and safe spaces."

Rob Kaiser, author of *The Versatile Leader*
and *Fear Your Strengths*

"Destined to become one of the most important management books ever written, *FairTalk* teaches the skills required to build cultures of impactful feedback and great performance. Firmly rooted in science and research, the book is simultaneously authoritative, creatively written, easy to read and use and – something long overdue – just a little irreverent and tells it like it needs to be told. If you hope to become a highly effective manager or leader, this book is a must read."

Jason Jennings, *NY Times, Wall Street Journal* and *USA TODAY*
and bestselling author of *Think Big, Act Small,*
Less Is More and *The Reinventors*

Published by
LID Publishing Limited
The Record Hall, Studio 204,
16-16a Baldwins Gardens,
London EC1N 7RJ, UK

524 Broadway, 11th Floor, Suite 08-120,
New York, NY 10012, US

info@lidpublishing.com
www.lidpublishing.com

A member of:

BPR
Business Publishers Roundtable

www.businesspublishersroundtable.com

Printed in Great Britain by TJ International
ISBN: 978-1-912555-09-3

Cover and page design: Matthew Renaudin

SERGEY GORBATOV & ANGELA LANE

FAIR TALK

THREE STEPS TO POWERFUL FEEDBACK

LID

LONDON NEW YORK SHANGHAI
MADRID BARCELONA BOGOTA
MEXICO CITY MONTERREY BUENOS AIRES

CONTENTS

To our spouses, who understand us, support us, put up with us and, importantly, give us FairTalk when it matters.

READ
THIS
FIRST

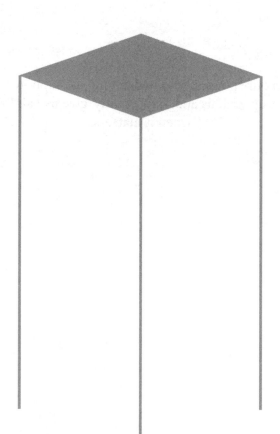

WHAT *IS* FAIRTALK?

First and foremost, FairTalk is about performance. It is the feedback that your team members need to deliver at the highest levels. This requires a continuous process of honest assessment coupled with a reason to, and accountability for, improvement. In that sense, FairTalk is aspirational. It is anchored in belief about human potential – your potential and the potential of every member of your team.

FairTalk, left at that, just wouldn't be very practical.

The aspiration of development gurus and self-help books must be tempered by what experience tells us and science confirms: we humans aren't very good at improvement. Instead of embracing honest assessment and the possibility of transformation, we're experts at avoiding feedback, rationalizing faults and launching into efforts to change, only to abandon them later.

So FairTalk is more.

FairTalk takes the science of why, as humans, we respond poorly to feedback and uses that knowledge. FairTalk deconstructs the reasons why feedback isn't given and why feedback, when it does happen, rarely works. It is a method for diagnosing individual performance issues. The result is a fair and focused assessment. A simple three-part FairTalk Statement *communicates* the needed change. The formula taps into the 'why' of change and then delivers an assessment of the current state of performance and expectations for improvement. The result is detailed, destination focused, developmental and – above all – doable (the 4 Ds) feedback. That's FairTalk.

By leveraging the science behind the FairTalk Statement, anyone can improve the performance of the individuals in their team.

However, performance improvement would still be difficult, and potentially unsustainable, if the efforts rested solely on your shoulders. FairTalk can be more than just feedback to an individual. FairTalk can become a culture: an ecosystem within the team, or the organization, where performance no longer depends on the manager's feedback to drive improvement. A simple diagnostic tool provides the basis on which the current culture can be assessed. Through the tool, the requirements for delivering a FairTalk Culture can be identified and implemented.

If that is what FairTalk *is*, it is only right to describe what FairTalk *isn't*. It isn't a formula to make employees happy, although it should make them satisfied. It isn't 'all about the dialogue' – it is tougher, and fairer, than that. It is about a clear expectation for change. The FairTalk approach isn't dogmatic. It is anchored in available research. As that evolves, we are open to feedback and change.

Finally, although FairTalk is simple, it isn't necessarily easy. But we'll teach you to master it. FIGURE I provides a summary.

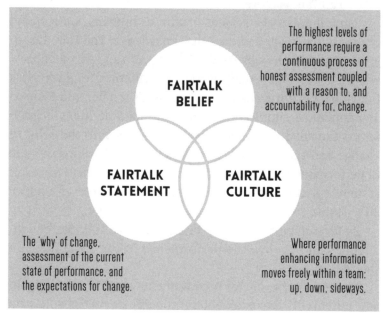

FIGURE I: What is FairTalk?

HOW TO USE THIS BOOK

You are busy. You don't need to follow the chapter sequence. Focus on what's relevant. Start with what matters most to you. You could even go to Chapter 15 right away to see the troubleshooting guide and work back from there.

PART ONE – FEEDBACK THAT MATTERS

We begin with the basics. In Chapter 1 we clarify the link between performance and feedback, debunking the myths unconfirmed by science. Chapter 2 talks about the science of human performance: capability, personal characteristics and context (we call these the 3 Cs). Chapter 3 points out the biggest barriers to progress. In Chapter 4 we uncover the foundational principles of feedback: fairness, focus and credibility. In Chapter 5 we lay out the compelling case for feedback. Today there is a heightened interest in the topic of feedback so we answer the questions 'Why?' and 'Why now?'.

PART TWO – FAIRTALK LEADER

This is all about what you need to *do*. If Part One is the theoretical primer on performance and feedback, Part Two is entirely practical. Chapter 6 will help you identify the specific developmental needs of your team and includes practical advice for confirming your thinking, for fairness and accuracy. A key reason feedback isn't given is that people don't know how to do it. At the heart of FairTalk is the Fair-Talk Statement, a straightforward approach to constructing effective feedback messages. Developing messages can and should be easy. Chapter 7 shows you how to develop an elegant FairTalk Statement that provides the learner with a reason to care, an honest assessment of their current state of performance and your clear expectations for the future. This practical methodology aligns with the science and is proven to add value in everyday coaching and in more formal performance appraisal settings.

In designing and delivering the FairTalk Statement we have also aimed to help you avoid three common traps. Chapter 8 concerns quality control for the feedback you plan to give. Feedback that is baffling, bogus or brutal (the 3 Bs) will do more harm than good. Chapter 9 deals with the emotional aspects of giving feedback. You'll learn how to 'keep calm and give feedback' through preparation and practice. Finally, Chapter 10 is all about the receiver. It will teach you to navigate contextual boundaries, such as culture, gender, generational differences or organizational layers, to connect with the receiver for improved outcomes.

Chapter 11 revisits the challenges of personal change. It deals with the questions of why change is tough but achievable. We are creatures of habit and habits can be cultivated. You will find out how to successfully build positive habits in those you lead.

PART THREE – FAIRTALK CULTURE

This is about shaping the organizational *culture*. By this stage, you'll know how to give feedback. You'll do it frequently and you'll do it well. But what about your team and those further down? A key step in building a FairTalk Culture is establishing clear expectations, providing the right tone at the top and instilling accountability for seeking and giving feedback (Chapter 12). Chapter 13 offers a diagnostic to assess your current state of culture, set a baseline and identify focus areas. Chapter 14 provides pragmatic solutions to help you create a FairTalk Culture in your organization. Chapter 15 is all about troubleshooting: evaluating the results of your efforts, gauging progress and taking remedial actions that will sustain your culture.

We pull together the key points of this book in the Conclusion, where we take one last look at the FairTalk Statement and the FairTalk Culture models.

At the end of each chapter you will find an interview with an expert. These experts comment on the subject matter. Sometimes, that is aligned to our approach. Other times, they bring a different perspective. That's okay. It's all feedback. And if, while reading this book, you also have a comment or a suggestion, please drop us a note. We love feedback.

PART ONE

Feedback That Matters

"Employees complain that they don't get enough feedback. So, the right question is, 'Why don't managers give it?' Some may believe it's optional. Or it doesn't work. But, dear manager, if you can meet your accountability to drive performance and alignment without feedback – good for you. You'll be the first."[1]

Lucien Alziari, chief HR officer, Prudential

If pilots fly planes and pianists play music – no questions asked, why don't managers do what they're supposed to? Give feedback, to be precise.

To figure that out, we conducted research to identify the key reasons why feedback remains scarce. Our work identified 21 separate reasons given by managers for not giving feedback. They included "I am not trained", "I feel awkward", "the employee will complain", "I don't know how to help them", "it's not my job", "my boss will disagree", "it takes too much time" and many other reasons.

We sorted what started as a random list into distinct categories. We could attribute every item to one of three reasons:

1. "I don't."
2. "I can't."
3. "I won't."

There were environments where there was no expectation to give feedback. There was *nil* accountability ("I don't"). So not giving feedback was the status quo.

Or, managers might lack the required know-how to give high-quality feedback, which is a lack of *skill* ("I can't"). A competence gap held them back from delivering the performance information their team members needed to hear.

Where there was a lack of *will* ("I won't"), it stemmed from either emotions or rationalizations. As it relates to emotions, giving feedback *is* an emotional experience for many of us. The rationalizations are potentially more problematic to explain. They might be unintentional. There might be what we consider skewed beliefs or myths about the impact of feedback. Or the rationalizations could be more harmful, stemming from bad leadership – for example, when a manager intentionally withholds feedback.

The result of our work was a simple decision tree:
The good news?
All of these reasons for not giving feedback can be mitigated.

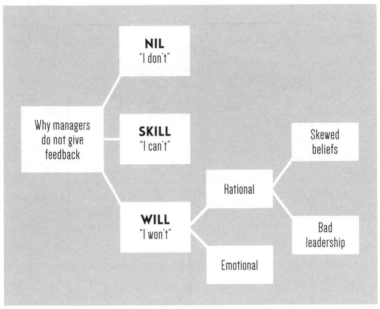

FIGURE 2: Reasons managers don't give feedback[2]

We'll tell you how. For starters, let's bust some myths around feedback.

CHAPTER 1

The Myths
Surrounding
Feedback

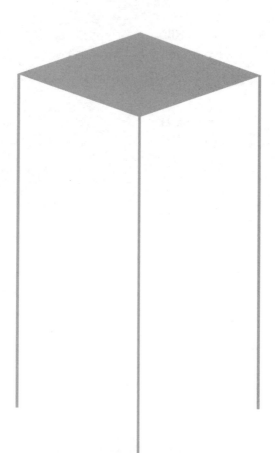

"Those who take management seriously – professional leaders – see giving feedback as a craft to be honed to the same sharpness as their technical skills."[3]

Jay Zimmerman, talent leader, Aon

There are few things that the management gurus are unanimous about. But they are unanimous about the value of feedback. It is conclusively proven. In fact, these days it is rare that a management speaker, consultant or business publication fails to mention the critical role of feedback in enhancing performance.

Yet the idea of 'feedback', even the mere word, makes us uncomfortable.

Which is odd, really, as we are introduced to feedback early on in our lives. Think back to your school days. Recall the tests, corrected by your teacher in strong, red ink (why is it always red?). That was feedback. We were okay with it. We understood that the person responsible for our learning would give feedback to help us improve. And we were right. A study at a leading UK university confirmed what we intuitively knew: getting feedback led to better performance by students. What's more, the researchers found that stronger students benefited even more from feedback than their less able classmates.[4] The same should be true for the world of work.

So why do we change our attitude towards feedback once we transition from there? After all, we embrace feedback in other aspects of our life. In fact, ratings are the new normal! In today's world, everything is rated. Feedback flows freely. Uber drivers and passengers rate each other, product ratings on Amazon influence what we buy, restaurants get instant feedback from TripAdvisor or OpenTable, and hairdressers can improve their service by checking their ratings on Yelp!

And, if we care about the ratings – that is, if we care about the feedback – we adjust our product or our service to meet the needs of our customers and clients. Surely we would want a lot of feedback, and the sooner the better.

So, what goes wrong in organizations?

SKEWED BELIEFS: FEEDBACK MYTHS AND REALITY

In society, it is the law (statutes and regulations), not intuition, that guides us. In a laboratory, validated methods determine the processes and the approaches that are used. Marketers base their strategies on market research. Unfortunately, this is often not true about leading others. Here, we often resort to gut feeling, assumptions, convenient interpretations, personal preferences and flavours of the day.

Organizations tend to believe things that are simply not true.

We believe it is these tendencies that contribute to the noise around feedback at work. In our review of the science of feedback, we found six common myths that managers hold about feedback.[5] These myths cause us to disregard a practice that has been proven to help others learn.

MYTH I: FEEDBACK HAPPENS ANYWAY

You should not believe: "Feedback is everywhere. Why should I get involved? They'll figure it out."

Ah, magical thinking. In a storybook, feedback, like the good fairy godmother, appears exactly when it is needed most. In the work context many leaders expect employees to somehow just... 'know'. The idea that feedback just happens has been refuted, time and time again, study after study. Managers typically do not give feedback. And it does not just magically occur.

MYTH 2: EMPLOYEES DON'T LIKE FEEDBACK

You should not believe: "People don't like feedback. Why should I add to their misery?"

Hardly a startling revelation that we don't like feedback! And indeed, there is evidence that people don't like feedback. Employees dislike it to such an extent that many will actually dodge feedback opportunities if they can[6] – and especially when there are performance issues. A study aptly titled "Are You Hiding from Your Boss?" discovered that in 24% of cases following a poor performance incident employees tried to avoid their manager.[7]

But this truth has been distorted to the detriment of employees and their performance.

First, each employee is different. Those who value feedback, are used to receiving it and are oriented on performance are much more likely to ask for feedback and act upon it.[8]

Second, what we *like* and whether we are *satisfied* are different. The correlation between *satisfaction with feedback* and *performance* is high and confirms that feedback can have an incredibly powerful, positive effect on performance. Conversely, dissatisfaction with feedback has a negative impact on performance factors, for example on accountability and confidence in doing a task.[9] In other words, performance improvements depend on satisfaction with feedback.

So, acting on a belief that "employees don't like it" throws the proverbial baby (the opportunity to improve performance) out with the bath water.

It's like an annual check-up with our dentist. We may not like the conclusion that we need a filling. But we ought to be satisfied that the diagnosis is thorough and accurate. And a skilled dentist can deliver the message without making us feel bad for not having brushed properly. Regardless of how 'happy' we are, addressing the problem is best. We are satisfied with the feedback and take corrective action. Smile!

MYTH 3: THE MANAGER IS THE ORACLE OF PERFORMANCE

You should not believe: "The pressure is all on me. I have to get it right. No one else can assess performance."

Most of us would accept that the role of the manager is critical. But, if asked to reflect, we would eventually agree that this is another half-truth. If there is lack of trust, employees may discount the feedback they get from their manager.

Research confirms that 'source credibility', or trust in the person giving feedback, affects the perceived accuracy of the feedback and the desire to respond, both of which affect subsequent performance.[10] When trust and personal engagement with your manager are low, feedback won't drive the desired outcomes.

Managers are important. But if, as a manager, you believe that the whole feedback ordeal is all down to you, two things are likely: you may miss out on finding inputs from a range of reliable sources, which could make the feedback both more credible and more accurate. Or, it will all just feel like too much pressure. After all, you might get it wrong...

MYTH 4: FEEDBACK IS GOOD; FREQUENT FEEDBACK IS BETTER!

You should not believe: "More is better!"

This is a case of "Yes, but." There is certainly evidence that frequent feedback is good. But can there be too much of a good thing?

An academic study demonstrated that there is a tipping point where an *increase* in the frequency of feedback leads to a *decrease* in task effort and performance.[11] This goes against the conventional wisdom that employees need a lot of it, especially as they are learning a new task or role. In fact, the same research confirms that too much feedback is particularly harmful at the early learning stage. Learning something new requires room for experimentation and learning from our own mistakes.

These results are supported by another study. In a field experiment, researchers manipulated the frequency and amount of performance feedback. They found that giving detailed information on how someone was doing led to a significant improvement in performance. However, it only served the purpose when provided over a sufficient period of time. When feedback was too frequent, performance was significantly worse than when detailed feedback was given less frequently.[12] Working on stuff takes time. Getting new information too often diffuses our focus and actually leads to a decrease in performance.[13]

MYTH 5: 'BAD' FEEDBACK IS... BAD

You should not believe: "I must give only positive feedback. Negative feedback causes conflict. Why would I want problems? And how on earth can I 'appreciate' bad results?"

There is a myth that negative feedback is bad. Maybe it stems from a fear of demotivating employees. Whatever the case, there is a misplaced idea that we should focus on 'appreciation'.

We like appreciation. There is nothing wrong with praise and recognition. However, the risk of dogmatically following the belief that 'bad' feedback is bad is threefold:

- Leaders avoid giving feedback altogether. We learn this early on from our parents: "If you can't say something nice, don't say anything at all!"
- Leaders sugar-coat the message. By the time they have turned the 'bad' feedback into something that is... well... not bad, it no longer has any practical value.
- Leaders deliver the message poorly. Leaders are notoriously bad at being feedback messengers: global data show that the skill of giving feedback constructively is at the bottom of the competency list of managers and executives.[14]

The idea that 'bad feedback is bad' is an example of a conveniently distorted fact. Research tells us that the nature of the feedback – that is, whether it is positive or negative – has virtually no effect on performance. Studies say that positive feedback may lead to a decrease in effort, just as negative feedback may boost a person's desire to achieve more.[15]

Performance is highly contextual. And, when feedback is properly situational, its bad rap evaporates. Robin Sharma, the author of *The Monk Who Sold His Ferrari*, tweeted that "Negative feedback can make us bitter or better."[16] You choose!

So, there are many factors that need to be taken into consideration in order to match the right message to the right person in a specific situation. Following are a few examples:

- Example 1: *positive feedback* can increase motivation when it is given to people who want to achieve, who take risks and who are sensitive to rewards (called a 'promotion focus').[17]
- Example 2: *negative feedback* can increase motivation when it is given to people who want to avoid trouble, who are generally cautious and who are sensitive to punishment (called a 'prevention focus').[18]
- Example 3: *negative feedback* can be especially beneficial in 'critical events', which are novel, uncertain, first-time situations where an individual cares deeply about the outcome, such as leading a new team or managing a crisis.[19]

The blanket belief that 'bad feedback is bad' aligns with most people's desire to avoid conflict. Instead, it is easier to believe that feedback needs to be motivational and uplifting. This may feel intuitively right. However, the evidence says that, while positivity and optimism may increase people's persistence in completing a task, they actually have an insignificant impact on performance.[20] Some scholars go as far as to say that "the only useful feedback is negative feedback". Others offer a softer perspective, saying that the motivational component of feedback can be positive or negative, depending on the person and the situation.[21]

As a leader, your job is to drive performance. You must provide feedback on what stands in the way. Helping employees temper their non-productive behaviours leads to a better mood at work, greater job satisfaction and stronger organizational commitment.[22]

We stand for focusing on things that matter. And, if that means delivering a few unpalatable messages to the altar of performance, then that's what we want to see. We strongly advocate for giving fair feedback, and, even then, it is because there are performance-based reasons for doing so.

MYTH 6: FEEDBACK IS THE PANACEA

You should not believe: "Once I've delivered the feedback, my work is done! They've heard me and are going to change."

This is another case of "Yes, but." A careful review of the facts affirms that simply providing feedback does not necessarily move the needle. An influential meta-analytical study demonstrated that only half of feedback interventions actually result in an increase in performance, while in a third of cases performance goes down after feedback.[23]

For your feedback to be in the half that increases performance, you have to take into account a variety of factors and synthesize them into a meaningful, high-quality message. You have to make that message relevant to performance and meaningful for the employee. You have to support the employee's improvement effort and provide feedback on progress.

The belief that 'feedback is the panacea' is a myth. 'Feedback is a powerful leadership tool that can help to drive performance' is the reality.

IN A WORLD WITHOUT MYTHS...

It is easy to see what happens when these myths take hold. You end up with something like what is shown in FIGURE 3.

As a good leader, I read management books and articles about feedback.

They tell me that...		And I'm thinking...
1. Feedback happens anyway		The world is full of feedback. It just happens naturally. No need for me to get involved...
2. Employees don't like feedback		...and moreover, most employees don't like feedback and avoid it anyway...
3. The manager is the oracle of performance		...but I'm the leader and it's up to me to deliver it. Nobody else can do it.
4. Feedback is good; frequent feedback is better!		So I take it upon myself to give my employees as much feedback as I can, very frequently...
5. 'Bad' feedback is... bad		...and I have to work hard to find a positive way of telling them that their performance needs to improve!
6. Feedback is the panacea		In the end, my hard work will reap great benefits. Once I have given them the feedback, their performance must go up.

But it doesn't... Is it any wonder I'm frustrated?

FIGURE 3: Six myths about feedback

So instead, let's imagine a world where facts rule.

In this world, we would want your employees to be satisfied, not necessarily happy, with thoughtful feedback. This fair feedback would have taken into account all the relevant information. You would have focused on what needs to change, not only on what they're doing right. They would hear the feedback and act on it because it's in their interests to do so and they wouldn't have necessarily been aware of the points raised unless someone credible had told them.

What keeps you from trying to create this world in your own team? Nothing.

KEY POINTS

Many managers, and organizations, embrace these six common myths about feedback. Acting on these myths can result in suboptimal results. Knowing the scientific facts about feedback will improve how it is given, creating more self-awareness in employees and contributing to better performance. Forming a point of view based on science will help you to avoid the risk of your feedback not achieving the desired impact.

EXPERT'S OPINION

FEEDBACK IS YOUR JOB

Lucien Alziari, chief HR officer, Prudential Financial, Inc.
Lucien has been chief HR officer at three major internationals: Avon, A.P. Moller-Maersk and, currently, Prudential. In 2018, Lucien won the prestigious HR Executive Award from the Academy of Management.

What is your personal relationship with feedback?

During my career, I was brought up with tough love, but it was always delivered with positive intent.

It's okay to be really tough with someone. But, if they don't believe you have their best interests at heart, you won't get anywhere. You will appear to be a jerk. If they feel you care for them, they will put up with any form of delivery. Just like relationships at home. Love is respectful, respect requires caring and caring is not necessarily being nice – it's doing what is best. Sugar-coating rarely is.

So, what is good "tough love" feedback?

One of the accountability principles managers need to follow is 'tough mind, soft hands'. You can't have wishful thinking when it comes to performance. That is what the organization requires. It is what people require. Call it what it is. How you deliver feedback is a very different matter. You can use "soft hands" to create a commitment. Perform two acid tests to see whether you did a good job and there is commitment from the other person:

1. Have I created commitment on the part of the receiver to do something?
2. Does the receiver have a choice about whether they are going to do something about the issue that has been raised?

You can't carry the burden if the other person doesn't act on the feedback. Your job is to manage the consequences, either way. The biggest trap is when, in the quest to help, you start doing their job; accountability shifts to the wrong place.

What conditions do we need to create so people get over their negative reaction to feedback?

Demystify it and make it a routine.

Too much feedback can become an emotional hurdle that makes it worse. Keep it manageable. Make it a ritual, a team practice, a matter of fact. Marc Effron suggests the 2+2 approach to feedback: each quarter you spend 15 minutes with each team member and tell them two things about their progress towards goals and two things that they should do differently.

The rules are the same for everyone, and they are clear and described up front. It is an agreement between the manager and the employee: everyone knows what to expect. It's simple and unemotional. It's not personal, not about you – everyone is doing it. Simple techniques like this take emotions out of it.

Will managers be more successful if they give good feedback?

It's good to remind managers that giving feedback is their job.

Organizations ask managers to manage people. Managers are accountable for driving alignment in their team, and across teams, and improving the performance of those they manage. They can't do this without speaking to people and having them course-correct along the way. In other words, if you don't give feedback you can't drive the performance that results in success.

But managers often don't feel comfortable. So you have to remind them what the manager and employee relationship is about. You are their manager, not their friend. It is good to have trust and be highly collaborative, but at the end of the day this is a professional relationship. The reason you are called a manager is that you manage your team's performance.

CHAPTER 2

About Human
Performance

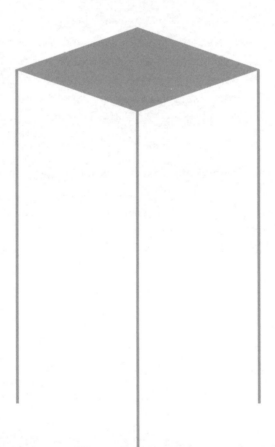

"You can raise the bar or you can wait for others to raise it, but it's getting raised regardless."[24]

Seth Godin

So you decide to be that leader. The leader who gives feedback anchored in science, who sets high expectations and who gets high achievement from the members of the team. To reach your high expectations, team members will need two things: the *capabilities* and *characteristics* to do the job. In both cases, their performance will also be impacted by the *context* in which the work happens.

To address any gaps in performance, it helps to understand why we perform the way we do – that is, why there might be a gap.

There is a body of research on human performance. In this book, we will touch upon only the few elements that are critical, and our goal is entirely practical. We are interested in those factors that you, as a leader, influence through feedback.

WHAT MAKES US PERFORM?
THE 3 Cs

Are there hard-and-fast fundamentals about performance that are constant?

These fundamentals that hold true for the leader-employee relationship. When these form the basis of feedback, it is fair and focused.

These fundamentals are:

- **Employers care about performance.** As the leader, you have the right to expect that employees perform at the optimal level. Performance is fundamental.

- **Performance is a result of both capability and characteristics.** It's both the *what* and the *how* of employees' contribution to organizational goals.
- **Performance outcomes vary based on context.** Context has a major impact on how goals are attained. It either facilitates or hampers performance.

To keep it simple, we call these the '3 Cs of performance': capability, characteristics and context (see FIGURE 4). Knowing these helps you to diagnose performance issues quickly and accurately.

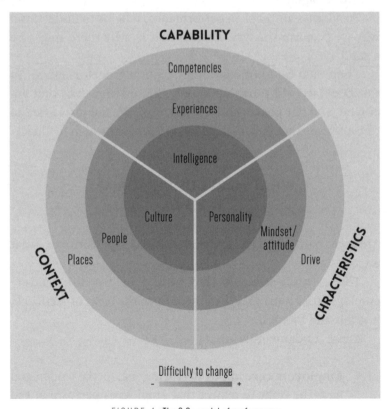

FIGURE 4: The 3 Cs model of performance

CAPABILITY

The first performance driver is capability, or *what* you bring to work to get the job done. Basically, it boils down to intelligence, experience and competencies – the knowledge and skills that you accumulate over time.

INTELLIGENCE

We want to mention intelligence, or more specifically 'cognitive abilities', here purely because of the large impact that it has on performance.[25] All other things being equal, an employee with a higher intelligence quotient (IQ) produces better results. This holds true across all levels of an organization.

EXPERIENCE

In the realm of performance, experience is king. No dose of sparkling personality, IQ score or conducive culture will compensate for a lack of relevant experience to drive a specific performance outcome.

Much of our performance has to do with our experience and how well we learned to do certain tasks over time. Here, we don't only mean technical or physical tasks. It can be knowledge work, such as strategic thinking or analysis. Our experience determines how well we go about executing the work.

Those who have gone through many varied, challenging and intense work experiences are likely to be better performers. They have accumulated knowledge and skills across diverse contexts and this greatly facilitates performance.

COMPETENCIES

Over time your experiences accumulate. As you *learn* from each experience, you build competencies.

A competency is something you need to be able to do well in a specific job role.[26]

We like this definition because it's simple.

Competencies can be technical (e.g. coding, or building a profit-and-loss statement) or behavioural (e.g. public speaking or giving feedback). Some are easier to develop, such as the ability to plan tasks. Others are more difficult to master. Building a shared vision, for instance, is a skill that is in short supply.

The absence of a competency may detract from performance. Sometimes the overuse of a competency may impede success. Many people are either unaware of these behaviours or unable to control them without your help as their manager (there will be more on this in Chapter 6).

If you need help thinking about the types of competency that someone might want to improve, you can use the FairTalk competencies, which are presented in TABLE I (page 39). These are based on our research and experience – try them out!

Alternatively, your organization may have a competency model. If it does, you should use it. Many consulting firms also have them. Any of these will help you to identify what's missing from your employee's performance. Competencies have different names and come in different flavours, but largely they are all the same stuff.

How would a member of your team know which of these skills it is most important for them to improve? How would they know whether they are overusing a skill? Or whether they are making progress? You've guessed right: the answer is feedback.

WHAT DO I DO IF THE ISSUE IS CAPABILITY?

Sometimes, when we ask the question "Can the person actually do this?" the answer may be "No" or "Yes, but not well."

As a leader, you have a unique vantage point. You know the baseline competence level of your employees. You know which skills individuals need to improve. An employee may think they are making progress when in reality their efforts are falling flat. They may even be practising a skill in the wrong way.

As a leader, you may be the closest person to the employee and thus able to observe and provide real-time information so that they can take corrective action.

When the issue is capability, performance feedback should emphasize the *actions* of building knowledge, experiences and skills.

CHARACTERISTICS

If capability is the *what* you bring to work, characteristics relate to *how* you go about doing your work.

PERSONALITY AND PERFORMANCE

Everyone has a personality. In simple terms, personality is the stable pattern of our behaviours. It is what we turn up to work with and includes such traits as how calm we are, how sociable we are, how easy we are to get on with, how dependable we are and how open we are to experience.[27]

But how do those affect performance?

When it comes to performing technical tasks, personality may matter less. Science agrees that the personality only has a moderate impact on tasks done individually.[28] However, this changes dramatically once work requires interaction with others. And it is especially true when leading others. As a leader, your personality accounts for nearly a quarter of your impact![29]

Depending on your personal characteristics, you will find some work easier and some harder. Consider this example: for an introvert, speaking up in a group may be difficult. We know there is no *physical* reason why an introvert can't speak up. Yet, not only does speaking up not come naturally but, in extreme cases, it may be hugely challenging. Compare this to an extreme extrovert. Not only is it possible for them to speak up but they may also positively prefer the opportunity to address the group.

Being punctual is another example. All of us, at least those who can tell the time, *can* be punctual in arriving at meetings. There are those, however, who shy away from planning. Punctuality just isn't wired into them. They can do it; it isn't a question of skill. But it takes more energy and mental bandwidth for them, compared to those who are naturally organized and plan well.

MINDSET AND ATTITUDE

In addition to having a personality (predisposition), you will have a point of view about your job, task and role. You can put someone in a job, but how that job is performed will depend on the mindset and attitude that the employee has. Strong capability and a great personality are not enough to bring about stellar performance in the absence of the right mindset and attitude.

The employee's mindset and attitude must be consistent with your expectations, as well as the organization's standards and values. For example, one of Amazon's leadership principles is Dive Deep, which means that "Leaders operate at all levels, stay connected to the details, audit frequently, and are sceptical when metrics and anecdote differ. No task is beneath them."[30] In this context, employees who don't get their hands dirty are likely to have tough performance conversations with their leaders about the right mindset and attitude.

DRIVE

Motivation and drive to perform are powerful predictors of performance. This is one of the best-researched areas in the social sciences. Employees with 'drive' will set or embrace goals. Here are five conclusive findings from the literature on goal research:[31]

I. The highest and most difficult goals produce the highest levels of effort and performance. Performance will only plateau or drop when it's no longer physically possible to carry on or when the motivation towards the goal wanes.

2. Setting specific difficult goals consistently motivates higher performance, compared to just urging people to do their best.
3. Goals must be personally important.
4. Individuals need to be confident in their own ability to reach their goals.
5. Feedback on progress towards achieving goals is critical.

Three major research findings supporting the importance of the last point – the feedback on progress – are as follows:[32]

- Hanna Klug and Gunter Maier reviewed a number of studies investigating the relationship between the pursuit of goals and measures of happiness (subjective well-being).[33] They found that progress against goals was more important than actually achieving goals in driving happiness.
- People's emotional responses (what psychologists call 'affect') to events that happen to them are determined by how they see these events impacting their progress towards their desired goals. Goal progress leads to positive affect and goal blockages lead to negative affect. And affect drives success. Research by Sonja Lyubomirsky and her colleagues shows that happiness is associated with and precedes many positive outcomes.[34]
- Finally, research by Teresa Amabile at Harvard Business School also reinforces the importance of progress.[35] Amabile and her colleagues studied employees working in 26 project teams in seven organizations over a period of several months. Employees completed diaries describing how they felt on a day-to-day basis and rated how engaged they were each day. When employees made progress, they reported more positive emotions, they were motivated by the work itself and they saw the work and their teams in a more favourable light.

In studies of motivation, psychologists distinguish between 'goal content' and 'goal striving'.[36] We've just talked about how the content of a goal influences drive. Now, let's talk about the 'engine' behind our effort and persistence – personal values.

Each of us has our own core values, which are deeply important. They could be about family, financial security, a need to do good in the world or anything else. By tapping in to what you know to be important to employees, you can unleash greater drive. You can better reframe their role or contribution in terms of what matters to them.

There are several values inventories and exercises that can be used to do this. Here is a simple one for you to try. Look at the word cloud in FIGURE 5. Select five values that are of central importance to you – that is, five values that determine what you love doing and how you prefer doing it. How do they show up in your day-to-day life? Would your team name the same five without you telling them?

FIGURE 5: Personal values word cloud

WHAT DO I DO IF THE ISSUE IS AROUND PERSONAL CHARACTERISTICS?

Remember, when we look at a performance gap, the first useful question is: "Can the person actually do this?" If the answer is no, we focus on building the necessary skills.

However, if the answer is "Yes they can" but they prefer not to, then performance feedback needs to create the right *expectations*. For example, "I know you don't prefer this, but my expectation is that you..."

This is explored further in Chapter 7.

CONTEXT

The final element of our performance model is context. Context is *the environment or circumstances* in which work happens.

Context can be positive (e.g. having a fantastic coach who greatly helps you along your way) or not (e.g. severe budget constraints). Think about driving a beautiful Ferrari down a dirt road in the countryside. The context (bumps and potholes) does not allow this car to realize its full potential to perform (fast speed on asphalt).

Context matters.

Harvard researchers studied the performance of surgeons who frequently perform operations in different hospitals, spending short periods of time in each hospital. They used patient mortality as a measure of success. The results were clear. The performance of surgeons depends heavily on the volume of their prior procedures at a specific hospital, regardless of the amount of work done at other hospitals.[37] In other words, experience in a specific context greatly facilitates performance.

Still at Harvard, another group of researchers examined the performance of top securities analysts who move to a new company. The analysts' roles, geographies and clients remained largely unchanged when they moved, and their performance success could easily be measured by the researchers (their personal rankings are published in public industry journals!). Invariably, the analysts' performance dropped for at least a few years following their change of company.[38] They needed to learn to perform in a new context.

The bottom line is that successful performance is highly context dependent. You can't have the same expectations of someone just learning a role compared to someone who has been in the role for three years. Similarly, an environment may be extremely conducive for someone to achieve great results without expending much effort.

There are many aspects to context. It could be budget. It could be market. It could be political stability... there are too many to outline. Context should modulate your feedback message, accounting for the headwinds and tailwinds your employee is experiencing. A smart manager takes all of these performance modifiers into account to deliver individualized and impactful feedback.

While there are many aspects of context, there are three that are *always* encountered. These three aspects are that:

- you work in a culture,
- you work with others, and
- you work in a physical environment.

I. CULTURE IS ALL AROUND US

The broader environment, or culture, impacts how we perform. It can be a force for good or not, as it relates to performance.

Sumantra Ghoshal, a renowned scholar and professor at the London Business School, delivered a speech titled "The Smell of the Place" at the World Economic Forum in Davos. He explained how the same employees will perform brilliantly or dismally depending on the environment that is created by their employer. He likened it to his vigour walking in the Fontainebleau forest in spring and great fatigue being in Calcutta in summer. He remarked with a note of sadness that many companies create downtown Calcutta within themselves.[39]

Most companies have a mode of culture. It may be a value statement, a competency model or similar. To the extent that this exists, even if it is aspirational, smart leaders use it when giving feedback.

Conversely, asking an employee for behaviours that are counter to the company culture is difficult. Let's imagine that you expect your employees to challenge the status quo in a traditional culture. If you are asking an employee to buck the prevailing culture, you must temper your performance feedback to account for that.

2. PEOPLE

Peers... can't live with 'em, can't live without 'em.

Within the margins of the behavioural range that is our personality, we will flex depending on those around us. We are social creatures. This can be a strong positive for performance – or not. As a leader, you have a great opportunity to make this a force for good. David Morrison, former chief of the Australian Army, famously said, "The standard you walk past is the standard you accept."[40] The standards you set, and importantly hold, for your team influence each and every other team member.

3. PLACES

Before deciding to give feedback, it is worthwhile to ask whether an employee is behaving in ways that are consistent with their peers. A good, hard look at those may act as a check on your feedback. You, as a leader, have a responsibility for the team. Borrowing an example from above, if a team member is continuously late for meetings but their peers is that meetings rarely start on time, the type of feedback, and the audience, need to change. In teams where everyone wanders in during the first ten minutes and there is no clear meeting purpose or agenda, the collective norm needs to be addressed first, and only then individual behaviours.

If you don't recognize the impact of the behaviour of others, two things will follow. First, the singled-out employee may rightly feel disenfranchised, and, second, you will miss the opportunity to realize the bigger performance opportunity of getting all meetings to be higher quality.

Before deciding to give feedback, it is also worthwhile doing a simple check on the physical environment and considering its impact on performance. As a leader, you have a responsibility for the physical environment, even though you may not always be able to do something about it.

If the workplace is noisy and full of distractions, feedback to an employee on the need to concentrate might need to be tempered. Similarly, you might adjust your feedback on quality of output if the equipment provided is old, faulty or in any way not conducive to quality. Or consider virtual work: connecting from an airport isn't as conducive to making a good contribution as being present in the conference room!

4. WHAT DO I DO IF THE ISSUE IS CONTEXT

Performance depends on the context, and the context today is increasingly complex. As a leader, you help employees manage it.

There is a concept in psychology called 'self-efficacy'. It is belief in your own ability to complete a task. "Yes, I can do it," is a good way to sum it up.[41] You must create this self-confidence in your employees. Before considering the feedback you will give them, reflect on how you influence their performance:

- Have I brought my team members on board properly?
- Have I set specific and challenging goals?

- Have I set clear expectations on the *what* and the *how*?
- Have I clarified the tasks and made the context clear?
- Have I explained the consequences of good and poor performance?
- Have I reinforced my belief in my team members' capabilities?
- Have I appropriately provided performance support and feedback?

Your personal relationship with your employees has a vast effect on their performance.[42] And a productive relationship is what your company pays for, and it's what you need to deliver, as the leader of the team.

Now you know the 3 Cs of performance, they can be your levers to great results. They are also the filters you can apply to make your feedback more accurate and impactful.

The funnel shown in FIGURE 6 (next page) is a useful way to illustrate how much 'stuff' impacts how people perform and how you can improve your feedback.

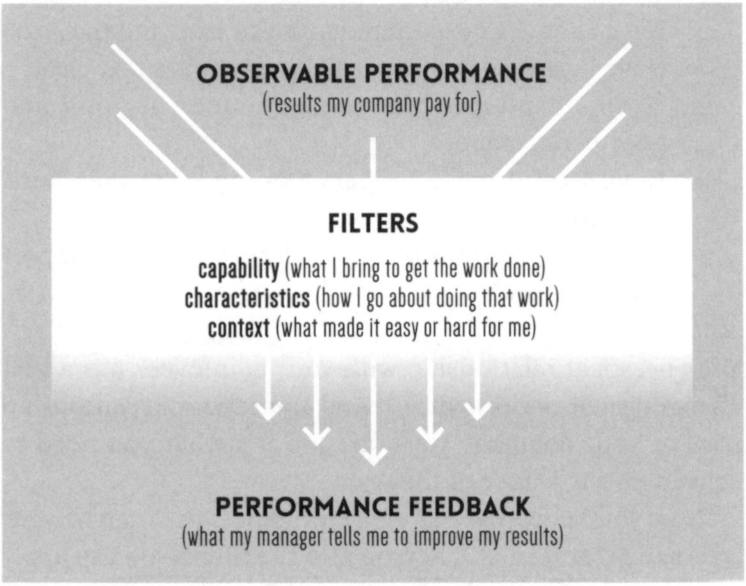

FIGURE 6: The feedback funnel

First published in Lane, A. M., & Gorbatov, S. (2017). Fair talk: Moving beyond the conversation in search of increased and better feedback. *Performance Improvement*, 56(10), 6–14. doi:10.1002/pfi.21731

KEY POINTS

Performance is a function of the 3 Cs: capability, characteristics and context. They determine how well we perform against goals and expectations. Giving feedback on progress towards those is a proven way to increase performance. Feedback is fair when it is *tempered* to take account of why performance is the way it is. People want to be treated fairly, and they respond well to fair treatment. The 3 Cs formula filters and crafts feedback to each employee's specific situation. Having considered why performance *is* like it is, the leader has insight into what needs to happen next.

TABLE I: FairTalk competency list: competencies for high

COMPETENCY	DESCRIPTION
Strategic	Anticipates the future. Plans ahead – implementing plans, allocating resources and removing roadblocks to not only respond to the likely changes but also take advantage of them.
Innovates	Connects, combines and invents the new and different. Encourages others to do the same. Evangelizes innovation. Balances innovation with pragmatism.
Functionally competent	Has the necessary skills and knowledge to be effective in the role. Stays abreast of recent developments in area of expertise.
Drives and delivers	Undertakes tasks with willingness and energy. Gets stuff done. Can be counted on to deliver on even the most challenging tasks.
Plans and controls	Approaches every task or project with an end in mind. Has a systematic approach to ensuring timely outcomes and making sure work Is efficient and resources are managed. Consistently monitors progress.
Decides	Makes high-quality, timely decisions, even when the situation is complex and ambiguous. Takes accountability for the decisions made.
Leads across the organization	Has the big picture of how the organization operates and is apt at connecting its different parts to ensure the greatest possible outcome for the whole company versus the success of individual parts. Creates and effectively manages internal and external networks.

Builds teams	Leads by setting a shared purpose, defining clear goals and aligning how team members work together to achieve results. Selects the right team members. Manages team relationships well.
Delegates	Manages work effectively by assigning full responsibility for tasks and projects. Follows up and provides necessary resources and guidance. Course corrects where necessary without micro-managing.
Sets vision and purpose	Creates a compelling picture of future success that the entire team and/or organization commits to. Engages others to follow the desired direction.
Motivates and inspires	Creates energy and enthusiasm for the vision. Builds an atmosphere where everyone feels engaged and driven towards that purpose.
Communicates	Effective in both written and oral communication. Conveys key messages across various audiences, tailoring the approach accordingly.
Leverages relationships	Understands the interests, motivations, pain points, etc. of others, and uses that knowledge effectively. Builds and maintains relationships with diverse groups of people.
Manages conflict	Embraces conflict as an opportunity to strengthen relationships. Surfaces interpersonal issues in a timely manner to resolve conflicts in the most effective manner. Not afraid to make tough decisions about people.

Influences	Able to influence a wide range of stakeholders to achieve an outcome. Effective at getting things done despite complex organizational structures or no direct authority.
Builds talent	Develops others through providing experiences, coaching and self-learning.
Gives feedback	Delivers relevant information about employees' performance and behaviours in a way that improves results.
Listens	Takes time to understand the views of others. Listens actively, asks probing questions and is genuinely interested in what others say. Lets others know they are heard.
Resilient	Keeps calm and composed, especially in high-intensity and stressful situations. Optimistic. Rebounds from setbacks quickly.
Patient	Controls the urge to speed things up to get to the closure. Adapts style between situations of urgency and those where 'haste makes waste'.
Knows self	Knows own strengths, limitations and feelings. Understands the impact these have on others.
Humble	Not arrogant. Values the opinions of others. Believes there are always opportunities to improve, while having the confidence to do so.
Loves feedback	Proactively seeks feedback. Non-defensive in receiving even critical opinions about self. Takes time to analyse feedback before acting upon it.
Learner	Eager to acquire new knowledge and skills. Learns from mistakes as well as successes, and applies that to future circumstances.

EXPERT'S OPINION

LEADERS VS. PROCESS: HOW ORGANIZATIONS UNDERMINE FEEDBACK

Elaine D. Pulakos, president, PDRI, an SHL company
Elaine is president of PDRI, which brings research and expertise to leaders around the world on topics such as performance and talent management, leadership assessment, skills development and more. Her latest book, *Transforming Performance Management to Drive Performance*,[43] talks about the important role of feedback in modern-day organizations.

What enables high performance, and how are we doing?

Years of research show that performance is best enabled and employees are most engaged when they know what to do and where they stand, and receive coaching and help to resolve performance blockers.[44] While seemingly simple, this idea has proven extremely challenging. We hear that the number one challenge is leaders' inability to give good feedback. We presume that addressing this will solve the biggest performance issues. Yet the way organizations run their people processes makes it hard and confusing for leaders to give good feedback. Organizations:

- disconnect people processes (such as performance appraisal) from work;
- make leaders the 'bad guys' by failing to teach them how to identify root causes;
- ignore environmental impacts on performance;
- forget the team.

So how can we help leaders to drive performance?

First and foremost, we need to connect people processes to daily work. Typical organizational systems pull expectation setting, feedback and coaching into separate steps that sit outside work, are scheduled and occur infrequently. To be effective, these activities need to be embedded in 'how work gets done', so they become contextualized and routinized.[45] At its core, managing performance is about repeatedly and fluidly setting expectations, measuring progress and course-correcting to achieve goals.

Leaders also should be leveraging naturally occurring performance information. There is no shortage of performance measures (e.g., customer satisfaction, delivery times, engagement scores). These exist but are underutilized, in spite of their advantages. Tracking a range of performance measures enables progress in real time, and these measures provide direct feedback. This takes pressure off managers, shifting their role from being sole evaluator and judge (bad guy) to helping the team interpret, prioritize and act on performance indicators. This enables managers to provide credible, informed and accurate feedback that facilitates meaningful performance dialogue and problem solving.

Are there aspects of the feedback process that leaders often overlook?

The importance of the environment is woefully ignored, despite the fact that the environment is often the culprit of substandard performance. We focus on setting goals and individual accountability as if each employee had full control over their results, which is rarely the case in today's matrixed, collaborative working environments.

The same goes for the role of teamwork. Technology and fast-paced change have brought more complexity to work, moving delivery from individuals to teams.[46] Employees may serve on multiple teams with different managers. In many cases, goal setting, performance measurement and rewards naturally sit at the team level. We talk about the importance of teams, but people practices haven't caught up.

CHAPTER 3

Why Improving
is Tough

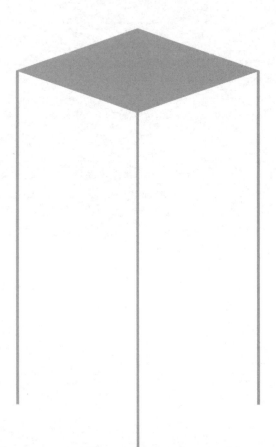

"Verily the lust for comfort murders the passion of the soul, and then walks grinning in the funeral."[47]

Khalil Gibran, *The Prophet*

You now have the 3 Cs as a lens through which you can pin-point why performance isn't happening as you expect. Now that you have that information, can an underperforming team member improve?

We believe that everyone is capable of some improvement and that feedback is an indispensable tool for any leader wanting to help employees get better at their job. But such improvement does not often happen. Why?

In our experience, there are three common reasons why people fail to improve in areas that you can influence. These are:

- low self-awareness;
- insufficient motivation to change;
- the strength of habit.

To keep things simple, we call these "I don't know", "I don't care" and "I can't change".

LOW SELF-AWARENESS, OR "I DON'T KNOW"

The fact is, most of us are not very good at self-awareness. Self-awareness is the extent to which we are *conscious* of our own behaviour, motivations and feelings, and conscious of the effect these have on others.

Many of us have blind spots – areas where we overestimate our abilities. This is called the 'above-average effect' and it describes the human tendency to overestimate our performance and our leadership abilities (and, as it happens, our health).

This principle was demonstrated, humorously, in a famous study that found that 93% of American drivers believe that they are better than the average driver.[48] Statistically tough, we know...

An inaccurately high perception of your own ability means weaknesses go unchecked and, if left unresolved, can derail performance or even a career.[49] In other words, delusions of grandeur will do you in.

And it gets worse! Research using fMRI data showed that being under pressure or cognitively overloaded increases this above-average effect.[50] If being under pressure and stress sounds like just another day at the office, then your risk of inaccurate self-awareness is high.

You would think the answer to overestimating our abilities would be hard data, right? Not necessarily. Even when we have objective measures of reality, we still misjudge how we are performing. In a three-month study of sales associates in a retail store, researchers correlated actual sales data, actual performance ratings and employees' self-assessments.[51] Not surprisingly, the employees' performance ratings were significantly correlated with their sales. However, there was no statistical relationship between the employees' self-evaluation and the sales-based ratings of their supervisors!

This problem is more widespread than you might think. An in-depth analysis of more than 100 research articles found that self-ratings of performance were higher than supervisory ratings by one third of a standard deviation.[52] In simple terms, that's a lot. Some researchers believe that only 10–15% of people are truly self-aware.[53]

In the absence of awareness, an employee is unlikely to self-correct. "Nothing resists change more than positive self-delusions: if you believe you are great, why would you want to change?" reflects psychologist Tomas Chamorro-Premuzic.[54]

While we are not good at seeing performance gaps in ourselves, we often see performance gaps in others. When asked to identify development opportunities in others, we overwhelmingly identify gaps such as listening skills, ability to delegate, the need to be inclusive or the need to be more open to change. Yet, the same people identify very different opportunities for themselves. They select 'gentler' items: the need for more focus, to have a better work-life balance or similar.[55]

The answer to "I don't know" should be easy. Provide feedback – in other words, deliver 'self-awareness', stand back and watch improvement happen! But we rarely do this. Why?

First, if you can't see it, you can't see it. Being told you have a gap may not be practically helpful if you don't accept that there is a problem to act on.

If this were the only problem, the solution would be clear. We're all about performance. Your employees don't have to agree with the feedback to act on it. So, as a leader, you'd insist on improvement and that would be enough, right? Still not that easy.

The very same lack of self-awareness that means we don't see the issue may also mean that we are not able to self-monitor our progress. We may not be good at assessing our own attempts at change. Poor self-awareness may then impact our ability to decide which attempts to change are more, or less, successful. The feedback loop, in other words, is faulty.

And that isn't the worst of it. Who are the people most likely to have issues with self-awareness? You guessed it! Poorer performers are the ones most likely to have blind spots.

Some people are born with, or learn, accurate self-assessment. As a result, these folks are inherently likely to perform better. There is scientific evidence that shows people whose self-evaluation aligns with the evaluations of others also tend to be higher performers.[56] In other words, the very people you probably need to give feedback to most are also the most likely to have a harder time using it. Sorry about that!

INSUFFICIENT MOTIVATION,
OR "I DON'T CARE"

Let's assume that an employee has heard your feedback. And they believe you, because you're a credible person to them. Believing you and being motivated to act on your feedback are *not* the same. If the employee thinks it doesn't really matter, they just may not care enough to change.

Most people want to do a good job. If you can explain why something matters, we believe most people would rather improve than not. A leader should be able to articulate why a behaviour or skill is important. In fact, if you can't state why a behaviour or skill matters to performance, it may not be worthy of feedback. It may be your preference or opinion, but if it doesn't impact performance, it is not worth worrying about.

So, starting with why the change is important, in terms of business outcomes, provides employees with a fair (we are all about fairness) opportunity to *decide to care*. You engage the employee in their own case for change by helping them connect the change to what is important or 'why it matters'. By telling your employee, "Consulting with peers before taking decisions is critical, as it improves decision quality and makes implementation easier," you have signalled the importance of the behaviour. Knowing that, the employee can either decide to try to change or not.

"This is why it matters" is powerful. It appeals to those motivated to succeed at work. It appeals to those who want recognition and those who respect hierarchy. It works for those who connect success to financial achievement. But it may not engage everyone as a call to action.

In some cases, despite identifying the critical reasons why change is needed, an employee may still not be motivated to try. You can lead a horse to water...

If a compelling 'why it matters' doesn't stimulate the employee to care, then:

- Check for **values**. Are you asking for something that is against the employee's core values?
- Check for **accountability**. Is the environment 'consequence free' for those not acting on feedback? More on this later.
- Check for **confidence**. Maybe the employee doesn't try because they don't believe they can succeed. They sabotage themselves. They don't try, and the prophecy is self-fulfilling.

When your employees lack motivation to change – that is, they 'don't care' – it is likely you will fail in your efforts to raise their performance. At that point, your role as a leader is to figure out what you'll tolerate. Lucien Alziari, chief HR officer at Prudential, confirms:

If someone is fundamentally not interested, there is little place for them in a modern organization. Because of how work gets done now, standing still is not an option. If you can't improve, it catches up with you.[57]

THE STRENGTH OF HABIT, OR "I CAN'T CHANGE"

The biggest impediment to improvement is likely to be habit, or inertia.

Our behaviours, good and bad, have developed over time. Much of what we do is not conscious. Our brain is so sophisticated that it takes over, allowing much of what we do to be done on autopilot.

The problem begins when we want to do something differently. Like improve.

We are motivated to get started but we quickly fall into comfortable, old routines and patterns. Our efforts to change are stifled. Willpower, or making ourselves behave consciously, is tough to sustain. And, while new evidence suggests that some of us are better than others at personal change, most of us are not good at it. Sustaining the new is particularly hard.[58]

Even the self-aware, motivated learner has to deal with the power of habit. But what does this mean for you as the leader?

Your role is to provide feedback. But, more than that, you need to deliver feedback in such a way, and with the required regularity and follow-up, that employees build *new* habits. Your role is to turn a performance gap into a practicable skill.

IF IT WERE THAT EASY, THEY'D HAVE IMPROVED BY NOW!

TABLE 2 summarizes the reasons we don't change and foreshadows some solutions that you can use to help employees improve.

TABLE 2: Three reasons people don't change

SYMPTOM	DIAGNOSIS	SOLUTIONS
"I don't know"	Low self-awareness	Tell 'em (Chapter 7), and tell' em usefully (Chapter 8). You could also direct the learner to other self-awareness tools, such as a 360-degree assessment or a personality assessment.
"I don't care"	Insufficient motivation	Find a powerful personal 'why it matters' so that the person chooses to care (see Chapter 7).
"I can't change"	Strength of habit	Replace bad habits with good ones and make them sustainable (see Chapter II).

Knowing the challenges that make change difficult – "I don't know", "I don't care", "I can't change" – allows you to adjust your feedback and follow-up. This gives your employee the best possible opportunity to improve their performance, and gives you the best possible opportunity to have a high-performing team.

KEY POINTS

Improvement is hard. Three issues impede improvement: when people can't see the problem, when they see it but are not motivated to act on it, and when they see it and want to change but can't seem to do so. Because improving is hard, the role of the leader is to move the employee beyond these hurdles in the service of team performance.

EXPERT'S OPINION

FEEDBACK AND PERSONAL CHANGE

Dr Tomas Chamorro-Premuzic, chief talent scientist, Manpower
Tomas is an international authority on psychological profiling, talent management and people analytics. He is the chief talent scientist at ManpowerGroup, professor of business psychology at University College London and visiting professor at Columbia University.

Can people develop?

Absolutely. We are never the same. Each morning we wake up with new connections (and old connections gone) in our memory and brain. The bad news is we are not necessarily in control of the change. After a certain age, changes are hard to make and small. And we often change for worse, rather than better. For example, you can expect more change as it relates to expertise or knowledge than you can turning people into a better version of themselves. Finally, a great deal of change can be predicted from an early age. This suggests ability to change is fundamentally a part of people's potential: for instance, people who are curious and humble will develop into better leaders, and vice versa.

How hard is it to develop, and why?

We are creatures of habit. Habits don't just take time to form – they take a long time to break and replace. As we get older, our desire to minimize behavioural choices and decision making drives us to become a product of our own 'default setting' – the automatic, instinctual, autopilot way of living life. To make matters worse, success reinforces our habits. The older and more successful we are, the harder it is for us to change.

What is the role of feedback in the development process?

It is instrumental. Without feedback, there is no awareness of the need to change, and particularly negative feedback can make people uncomfortable by highlighting a gap between the person they are and the person they want to be. Although this doesn't automatically translate into effective change, change won't happen without it.

What role do our personality or values play in how easily we develop?

Although personality and values are very stable, they dictate how and why people change, respectively. You can trigger change by asking people to do things that are congruent with their natural style (personality) and by motivating them around their core beliefs (values). In fact, people will experience the *urge* to change if you make them realize that they are going against their nature or doing something that is incompatible with their belief system. But you often need to make this very clear to them, which is where feedback matters again!

How do our personality or values affect how we give feedback?

They play a big role. On one end, you have people who are curious, humble, eager to learn, data driven and self-aware. They will master the art of requesting honest and critical feedback and make the most of such valuable information. On the other extreme, you have people who are arrogant, entitled, narcissistic or defensive. They will not only shy away from getting feedback from others (particularly negative feedback) but also be immune to it when they get it. They are, in plain terms, pretty un-coachable.

CHAPTER 4

Foundational Principles of Feedback

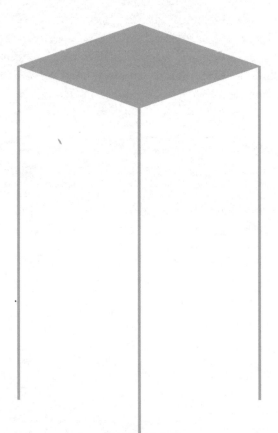

"Being good is easy, what is difficult is being just."[59]

Victor Hugo

You are committed to performance and improving the self-awareness of your team members. You want to motivate them to positively grow through new, productive habits.

This happens when your feedback is heard and acted upon. For this to happen, it must meet three critical prerequisites: *fairness*, *focus* and *credibility*. When these conditions are met, it's FairTalk.

FAIRNESS

Fairness means taking into consideration the employee's capabilities, their personal characteristics and the business context before deciding that they need to improve their results. In other words, it means considering the situation holistically before you diagnose and give feedback.

We all want to be treated fairly. Being treated fairly increases self-esteem, sense of belonging and overall satisfaction, all of which have strong positive relationships with performance.

Moreover, fairness makes us:

- **Happier.** In an experiment, participants were dealt a mix of fair and unfair monetary offers. Not surprisingly, those who got a fair deal reported feeling happier. What was insightful was that the brain activity of individuals receiving unfair offers was similar to the brain patterns observed when we face a major negative event.[60] Happier people may, or may not, perform better. But no one performs at their best after a major negative event!
- **Engaged.** Burnout is the opposite of work engagement. There is evidence that employees experience less burnout

when they are assessed fairly.[61] In a study that specifically focused on feedback fairness, when employees got fair feedback, they were more likely to be satisfied with their job and less likely to get depressed.[62]

- **Loyal**. The perceived fairness of feedback has a negative relationship with an employee's intention to leave the company.[63] If I think your feedback is fair, I won't quit. Even when times are tough, fairness pays off. In a study of over 11,000 people, scientists found that fairness in downsizing decisions was strongly correlated with a positive attitude towards the organization. And this was true for both those who stayed and those who were let go.[64]

So, how do you make feedback fair?

BEWARE OF BIASES

We flag bias here because unbiased feedback is key to fairness. (There is a detailed discussion of how to increase the accuracy and fairness of your message in Chapter 6.)

USE FEEDBACK MODIFIERS

As noted, start by taking into account the circumstances around the performance. These factors act to *modify the feedback* you give. For example, your feedback would be different for two employees with the same results if one were new to the role and the other a seasoned pro.

Before sharing your observations, filter for the 3 Cs – capability, characteristics and context – and then formulate your feedback.

Elaine Pulakos, president of PDRI, states:

I advocate for evaluating the context first – a step that most of the time gets under the radar of leaders. Our general failure to direct leaders to environmental blockers misses the root cause of many performance issues.[65] *The remedy is to teach leaders to diagnose situational barriers first, before looking to individuals, in diagnosing performance failures.*[66]

Additionally, before sharing your feedback, you will need to check it for consistency. Ensure that it targets the outcomes you want. And use language that is non-judgemental and assume positive intent.

BE CONSISTENT

It is common sense (and also supported by research) that consistency in evaluations is a strong predictor of perceptions of fairness. Consistency doesn't mean treating everyone alike. In this context, it means interpreting the same set of modifiers similarly.

To do this, make sure that there are "constant, clearly established, explicitly stated feedback standards that are always known and consistent across employees".[67] You may have an HR team that enforces performance ratings definitions and conducts calibration sessions to try to bring that consistency. Be kind to them! They know that consistency is part of what makes us feel that the process is fair.

FEEDBACK ON WHAT AND ON HOW, NOT ON WHO – IN OTHER WORDS, IT'S NOT PERSONAL!

Fair feedback targets the outcomes and behaviours, not the person. The moment we perceive that our self-image (ego) is under threat, our brain fires up to tackle that threat.

We start to get creative about finding ways to uphold our self-image or to manage the impressions of others. We rationalize (e.g. "Here are five reasons why it's not my fault"), we deflect (e.g. "This is not the real issue we must deal with here"), we enhance (e.g. "My project results are so much better than everyone thinks!") and more.

Our mental bandwidth is absorbed and our attention diverted from the task at hand: processing feedback that would enhance our performance.[68] As a leader, your role is to cut through the defensiveness and establish your expectations for the future.

You must deal with both the *what* and the *how*. By focusing on work results and how those were achieved, you stay at the performance level. By focusing on the observable behaviour and not on the personal characteristics, you reduce the risk of triggering those emotions. Employees will be less defensive.

So, if you hear an employee trying to avoid, deflect or refute the message, emphasize the current work output or behaviours.

ASSUME POSITIVE INTENT

Another step towards increasing fairness is to assume the employee had positive intent.

Additionally, you should have the intention to be positive: you are giving feedback, so the chances are you are in a position of strength relative to the feedback receiver. So, no need to be a jerk, right? We can all be respectful, even kind, without excusing the behaviour or the result. Have the intention to say what needs to be said, so the employee can improve.

And, as well as being humane, it turns out that this is good business sense.

People respond not only to what they hear (e.g. "Here is what I think of your work") but also to the intent of the action (e.g. "I want you to be successful in your job").[69] Research shows that being gentle, caring, respectful, courteous and sensitive in communicating feedback greatly increases the perceptions of fairness.[70] Carl W. Buehner perhaps said it best with: "People will forget what you said, people will forget what you did, but people will never forget how you made them feel."

Executives and leadership gurus agree. Here's what we heard from the chief HR officer of Prudential, Lucien Alziari, when we interviewed him:

For the whole relationship to work, assume good intent. This needs to be true on both sides. It's tough for a meaningful performance conversation to happen without this being stated, re-stated and re-stated again. Keep reminding people about the context. Reinforce that it is well intended and not an exercise in finding faults. It forces you to confirm the relationship and creates the environment you live up to. If the receiver thinks that you are political or manipulative, it doesn't matter how technically pure you are – you have lost the message anyway.[71]

And, at the same time, assume that the employee has good intentions too. Rob Kaiser told us:

Unless you have strong evidence to suggest otherwise, assume positive intent. Most employees do not perform poorly on purpose; more often they simply don't know better or how to do better. Begin the conversation with the positives ("I know you are trying to do a good job...") and show that you understand the person and her strengths ("I have observed that you are really good at..."). It is a truism in development that people are more willing to take your advice if they believe you understand them and what has made them successful.[72]

Assume the person started off from a good place, wanting to make a positive impact. And remember the modifiers, such as: *Were there significant headwinds? Did the person get the right skills and resources?* and *Did something significant happen in the employee's personal life?*

And then kindly, but clearly, tell the person what they need to hear.

MAKE TIME

Most recent research shows that leaders who choose business tasks over people matters come across as being less fair.[73] Your schedule is already overbooked. But it's your choice what you overbook it with. Just be cognizant of the trade-off between meeting deadlines and appearing fair to your team.

FOCUS

If you fire a shotgun at a target and you are lucky, one of the pellets will hit the mark. The spread is wide. Hitting the sweet spot is not guaranteed. A rifle, on the other hand, is a different matter altogether. It's just one bullet going straight for the bull's eye.

Focus is the difference between the shotgun and the rifle.

You may pray that your feedback will land where you plan. But you are pressed for time and have limited opportunities to engage team members. You have to make your messages hit the target. So, they must be focused... otherwise you might shoot yourself in the foot!

FairTalk is like a rifle shot.

There are myriad things to give feedback on, but not all of them weigh equally on performance. Choose only what matters. Conveying too much information just blurs the focus.

Focus also ensures greater accuracy. If we perceive feedback as accurate, we are more satisfied with it. And it is the satisfaction with feedback that significantly influences performance.[74]

There is a paradox to be aware of. Science tells us that the best feedback is both specific and generic. More often than not, you would want to provide your employees with focused feedback on what needs to improve, while being generic about the solution, so you leave them enough freedom for creativity and exploration.[75]

A study was conducted with two groups of students who took part in a computer simulation. One group received generic feedback on their people-management decisions and the other more specific feedback. The group that received detailed feedback did better on the task, but the group that received generalized feedback had to think more and therefore demonstrated a greater degree of competence *after* the simulation. The specificity increased task performance, while the generic direction increased learning.[76]

In practical terms:

- When giving feedback, go for *specificity*. Point out the exact behaviours that need to be improved, using facts and concrete situations from the recent past, and relate them to customer or peer feedback, if available.
- When coaching, raise your comments to the more *generic* level. Encourage employees to consider what the best experts in the company or industry might do, link individual results with the firm's strategy and ask open-ended questions.

In Chapter 7 we will talk about this transition from feedback to coaching. But feedback must come first. A combination of specific feedback and reflection results in both improved performance and more learning. Reflection on its own, without feedback, has no impact on performance.[77]

CREDIBILITY

Research strongly links the credibility of the feedback source to performance. Feedback that is not seen as credible is less likely to be acted upon.[78] Credibility determines whether your employee will listen to feedback and act on it.

For most of us, the feedback we need to provide team members with is based on our own opinion. It is therefore likely to be subjective. Even the most objective measures of results have an element of context that colours them. And that's okay.

First, as a leader, your job is to make subjective judgements. Don't feel bad that they are subjective. Assessing performance is part of your role. You are paid for your professional opinion.

Second, typically people won't take your judgement as fact – unless you are credible to them. When you are, your feedback is perceived as objective anyway![79]

We believe the need for credibility is on the rise. In Chapter 5, we will discuss the megatrends shaping the modern workplace, but here's a sneak preview:

- **Blurred line of sight.** When you can't see the work or the worker, your credibility as a judge of performance is lower.
- **Erratic environment.** The rising demands on your time and capacity leave less space to establish trusting relationships with your employees.
- **New worker deal.** Lower employee loyalty and frequent job moves take a toll on your credibility as leader.

Being credible makes your feedback more effective. Credibility is also increasingly difficult to achieve.

According to the 2018 Edelman Trust Barometer,[80] trust globally is at its all-time low. The numbers are down from the previous year, and the 2017 report was titled *Trust in Crisis*!

Here is an example of an uncomfortable finding from the 2018 report: 60% of respondents believe that CEOs are driven more by greed than by a desire to make a positive difference in the world.

Why do we trust the opinions of people we don't know (such as reviews on Glassdoor, TripAdvisor or Airbnb) while holding deep distrust of someone who is paid to ensure that we perform at our best? Surely they have at least a pragmatic interest in our growth and development?

You are up against some strong negative stereotypes about leadership. The TV series *The Office* and *Dilbert* cartoons are sad (but brilliant!) examples of such preconceptions. Anecdotes relating to managerial incompetence, abuse of power and just plain bad leadership are everywhere. They spread scepticism. And scepticism gnaws at credibility.

WHAT EXACTLY IS CREDIBILITY?

A comprehensive and practical view of credibility is that it is a sum of competence, goodwill and trustworthiness.[81] That is, do you know what you are talking about, how much do my interests matter to you, and can your opinion be trusted?

Try out the simple assessment of credibility below. Or ask your team members to complete it anonymously. Our bet is that, if there are issues in interpersonal relationships in your team, you will be able to pinpoint specific causes.

EXERCISE: MEASURE OF CREDIBILITY[82]

Please indicate your impression of the person you are assessing (it could be yourself) by **circling** the appropriate number between the pairs of adjectives below. The closer the number is to an adjective, the more certain you are of your evaluation.

Competence							
	Intelligent	1	2	3	4	5	Unintelligent
	Trained	1	2	3	4	5	Untrained
	Expert	1	2	3	4	5	Inexpert
	Informed	1	2	3	4	5	Uninformed
	Competent	1	2	3	4	5	Incompetent
	Bright	1	2	3	4	5	Stupid

Goodwill						
Cares about me	1	2	3	4	5	Doesn't care about me
Has my interests at heart	1	2	3	4	5	Doesn't have my interests at heart
Not self-centred	1	2	3	4	5	Self-centered
Concerned with me	1	2	3	4	5	Unconcerned with me
Sensitive	1	2	3	4	5	Insensitive
Understanding	1	2	3	4	5	Not understanding

Trustworthiness						
Honest	1	2	3	4	5	Dishonest
Trustworthy	1	2	3	4	5	Untrustworthy
Honourable	1	2	3	4	5	Dishonourable
Moral	1	2	3	4	5	Immoral
Ethical	1	2	3	4	5	Unethical
Genuine	1	2	3	4	5	Phoney

Sum up the scores for all the answers; the total should fall between 18 and 90. **The lower the score, the higher the perceived credibility.** Numbers closer to 90 mean someone is completely not credible. Do the tally for each of the three components of credibility. Is one score significantly lower or higher than the others? Why might this be?

Think about how each of these three elements (competence, goodwill and trustworthiness) relate to feedback that you give to your team.

COMPETENCE

People are more likely to accept feedback from someone with expertise. Even when the feedback is tough. A study of 216 supervisor–subordinate pairs showed that, when employees perceived their managers as experts, they valued their feedback more and were more willing to ask for negative feedback.[83]

Competence points can be gained through training and certification (all those plaques on the wall in the lawyer's or doctor's office...). But are you considered competent?

If you have been around the block, you may have a reputation for knowing what you are talking about. On the other hand, if you are new to the team, be proactive and transparent about your strengths and weaknesses. Surprisingly, just laying it out there adds to your leadership credibility.

Want another counterintuitive suggestion on increasing others' perceptions of your competence? Ask questions and seek advice. A group of researchers from Harvard University and the Wharton School at the University of Pennsylvania conducted a series of experiments proving that seeking advice from your team actually increases (instead of decreasing) how competent you are perceived to be.[84]

GOODWILL

Certificates are not given out to prove your goodwill, so it's down to communication and behaviours.

Consistently giving feedback is actually quite helpful in building goodwill:

- I spend time with you (= your performance is important to me);
- feedback is you-oriented (= I focus on how improving your performance will make you more successful);
- feedback is useful and fair (= I understand and want to help).

Just adding a little routine, consistency and structure can help to build a lot of goodwill.

FairTalk is inherently a builder of goodwill. When you apply the FairTalk approach to thinking about feedback – for example, by focusing on what matters most or recognizing circumstances or modifiers that impact performance – you are living 'goodwill'.

TRUSTWORTHINESS

This is perhaps the most difficult credibility element but it is also the most important. It is about walking the talk, keeping promises and living up to espoused values. And it pays off. When employees trust their supervisors, they are more likely to seek feedback from them, even if it is negative.[85]

Giving honest feedback actually makes you more trustworthy. Telling people the truth about how they perform, how the company views their contribution and career trajectory, and what they should do to become better is the right thing to do. It can be uncomfortable and emotional, but people will listen to you more when they know that you are being fair.

Consider the alternative. Not telling people where they stand in terms of performance and potential is akin to lying to them, according to Marc Effron and Jim Shanley, founders of the Talent Management Institute. This is not a great way to build trust.

We believe employees have a right to know how they are doing in key aspects of their professional life. And being honest about their career prospects is beneficial to the person and to the organization, contrary to what many managers believe.

It is true that someone may leave when told that their career path is at its peak. But they also may decide to stay and put all their effort into demonstrating superior performance at the current level instead of trying to get that illusory promotion. This may actually change the way that the company sees this person's potential.

In either case, goodwill and honesty win every time. As psychologist Tomas Chamorro-Premuzic asserts, "what people need is honest feedback on their potential, rather than confirmation of their talent delusion."[86]

KEY POINTS

Fair leaders select feedback that directly impacts performance outcomes, taking contextual and personal factors into consideration. Those are called 'feedback modifiers'. They temper the message to account for individual circumstances. Focused feedback channels employees' attention and energy to areas most critical to their performance. Credibility is a prerequisite for the feedback to have the desired effect. By enhancing their personal competence, goodwill and trustworthiness, leaders become more credible.

EXPERT'S OPINION

FAIR, FOCUSED AND CREDIBLE FEEDBACK IN THE WORLD OF THE NEW WORKER DEAL

> **Svetlana N. Khapova, professor, Vrije Universiteit Amsterdam**
> Svetlana is professor of careers and organization studies at Vrije Universiteit Amsterdam, the Netherlands. She has dedicated her life to understanding individuals' careers and their impact on the world. Together with her collaborators Michael Arthur and Julia Richardson, she shares her views on contemporary careers in her recent book *An Intelligent Career*.[87]

In today's environment, where employees move jobs and companies regularly, does the employee even care about getting fair, focused and credible feedback? In the traditional lifelong model of employment, receiving feedback from your manager on how you do in your job and in your career was sufficient. Today, receiving such feedback might mean at least two things.

One is that you must be doing well, if your manager is happy. But another is that you might need to reflect on whether what you learn in the job is still marketable and would make you employable outside the organization when needed. We call this thinking 'intelligent career'.

What is an intelligent career?

An intelligent career means the employee owns their own career. It may sound easy, but it is not easy at all. Pursuing an intelligent career means being reflective on your personal career situation. It means continuously asking yourself: Am I doing well professionally? Am I on schedule compared to personal goals and milestones? What else needs to be done, and which other experiences do I need to build a career profile that will help me to stay employable?

How do employees get the necessary feedback to support their intelligent career objectives, if not from their manager?

Employees also need to turn to a diverse career network for feedback. For example, what about talking to a father in your son's football club, who is a manager in an industry in which you aspire to progress? What about speaking to your former university tutor, who still watches your development through social media. What about talking to your partner or spouse, who often knows more about your talents than you do?

In today's environment, an employee's feedback network should include those who don't have any corporate agenda. These people are all around. Employees need to turn to their personal career network and start asking questions.

What do intelligent career seekers need to get feedback on?

An intelligent career relies on three career competencies (knowing *why*, knowing *how* and knowing *whom*) that you need to continuously invest in. These competencies need to be independent of your employer.

Ask *why* do you work? Think beyond the objectives of the organization.

Ask *how* do you work? This involves experiences and skills that are portable.

Ask *with whom* do you work? Consider co-workers but also clients, customers, suppliers, and business and non-business partners.

So an intelligent career might not be consistent with what the organization wants for you?

Yes. For example, receiving feedback that you could develop into a specific type of programmer or go on an international assignment might be good for the organization but less good for the employee. An intelligent career approach teaches that we need to focus on developing transferable – rather than company specific – skills and competencies, whenever possible.

CHAPTER 5

Why Feedback?
Why Now?
Why Not?

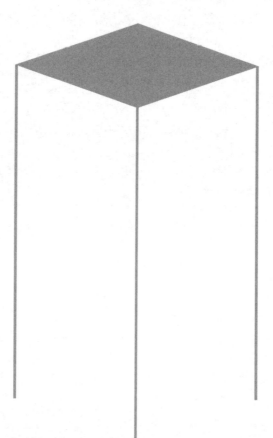

"I've come to believe that things are getting better and better and worse and worse, faster and faster, simultaneously."[88]

Tom Atlee, *Crisis Fatigue and the Co-creation of Positive Possibilities*

WHY DOES IT MATTER?

The sceptics ask, "Is feedback really an answer?"

Before jumping on that bandwagon, let's pause and consider the present and the future.

Think about your role and the challenges you face. Consider all the factors that affect your performance. What are the issues most impacting how your team delivers? Which of these is under your control? How will you deal with those?

Now, gaze into the future and reflect:

- What will the environment be like in the future? How similar? How different?
- If different, in what ways? Are you better off? Worse? Why?
- And, most importantly, what must you do now to prepare to be successful in the future?

As a leader, you want to do a good job. But the world of work has changed and somehow delivering results feels harder than ever.

At least you are not alone!

Agility, flexibility and disruption are the new normal. The working environment today is different from that of the past. For us, three differences stand out (see FIGURE 7 next page). We call these:

- blurred line of sight;
- erratic environment;
- new worker deal.

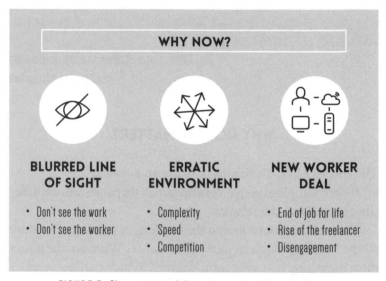

FIGURE 7: Characteristics of the contemporary working environment

BLURRED LINE OF SIGHT

WHEN YOU CAN'T SEE THE WORK BEING DONE, IT'S KNOWLEDGE WORK

Half a century ago, Peter Drucker described a world increasingly defined by knowledge work. He argued that the company's most valuable asset would be its knowledge workers. He was right.[89]

Not long ago, the tangible assets of a company equalled its value. Today, their contribution is close to negligible. In 2015, the value of *in*tangible assets accounted for 87% of the total valuation of companies within the Standard & Poor's 500.[90] Drucker predicted what we now know to be true. Intangibles, such as innovation, creativity and human performance, are at a premium today.

How do you, as a leader, improve performance when the raw material is information, when you can't see the production process and when the impact of any one individual on the business's results is, at best, indirect? How do you manage people when their work does not directly produce a result but instead contributes to it? How do you even assess 'contribution'? And how do you give feedback that drives the individual to improve that contribution when the line of sight you have to the work is blurred?

WHEN YOU CAN'T SEE THE WORKER

It is one thing not to see the work. But now, it is very likely you won't see the worker! Virtual work, working from home, distributed work, virtual teams – all these are a current reality. Companies approach them differently: some embrace these ways of working, others insist on more traditional and proven approaches, while still others try to retrace their steps, as exemplified by Yahoo's ex-CEO Marissa Mayer's memo on limiting virtual work[91] or IBM's CEO Ginni Rometty calling her virtual workers back to the office.[92]

Whatever the company's strategy, the trend is clear. And this brings new complications. Remote employees feel less supported and may feel 'left out'.[93] And leaders must figure out how to see, assess and improve their employees' performance in this virtual world. The pressure is mounting.

ERRATIC ENVIRONMENT

It was always going to be hard. But conventional wisdom suggests that at least two factors are making it harder: complexity and speed.

COMPLEXITY IS… MORE COMPLEX

Things certainly feel more complex. And, if the writings of management thinkers are anything to go by, complexity is definitely a 'thing':

Managing a business today is fundamentally different than it was just 30 years ago. The most profound difference, we've come to believe, is the level of complexity people have to cope with.[94]

The reasons for the growing complexity are many, but complexity has certainly been enabled by technology. Technology has increased the number of variables in any given situation while simultaneously reducing the time available to process them.[95]

SPEED IS… SPEEDIER

If complexity isn't difficult enough, the speed at which the complexity evolves and changes adds to the challenge. There is ample evidence that the acceleration of change is exponential, not linear. In the time it would take to grasp excellence in performance, the standards have likely changed.

'Just hanging in there' is no longer an option.

…AND BUSINESS IS GETTING TOUGHER

If you accept that complexity and speed of change are difficult, it still might be okay. If all companies face these issues in equal measure, there is no overall change to competitive advantage.

But that doesn't seem to be the case.

The same knowledge work that brings challenges also enables 'disruptors'. Like Amazon. Or Airbnb. Disruptors change whole industries. When the next Uber or Netflix comes for your industry, will you be ready? Companies built for agility, where communication flows freely to enable innovation, will be more prepared to face such intruders. Complacent companies are easier to disrupt. Leaders must strive to increase the performance of their teams where business is getting tougher.

NEW WORKER DEAL

Possibly because they are winning 'the war for talent' or possibly in response to the failure of organizations to provide job security, employees are also changing. Three trends in particular are worth considering.

THE END OF A 'JOB FOR LIFE'

Recessions, financial crises and social changes have made the notion of lifelong employment obsolete.

There is an emerging career reality. It goes by various names – boundaryless, Protean, intelligent, portfolio career, etc. Employees are taking ownership of their professional lives by pursuing greater employability inside, and outside, their current companies.[96]

A scientific review of contemporary career behaviours highlighted that, today, employees are increasingly likely to switch companies and seek alternative work arrangements, and less likely to enjoy either a swift vertical career climb or job security.[97] Many employees happily trade job security for more flexibility to balance work and life and for greater decision power in how and when they enter and leave the workforce.

And the very best talent is constantly on the lookout for better opportunities. A study of 892 high-potential early-career professionals found that:

Among individuals who were still in their first job, 92% of respondents reported that they were always on the lookout for opportunities with other employers. They revised their résumés, monitored job openings at other employers, talked to friends about job opportunities, or obtained information on prospective employers at least once in the year of our survey. Sixty-three percent applied for jobs, attended job interviews, or contacted search firms at least once in the survey year.[98]

The implications are clear. As a leader, you have less time to bring your employee up to the required level of productivity and to gain return on the investment. A *Wall Street Journal* article offers a take on modern-day employability:

Determined to retain your most talented executives? Well, here's some counterintuitive advice: The best way to keep them from leaving is to prepare them to do just that.[99]

THE RISE OF THE FREELANCER

Potentially due to the lack of a single job for life, or perhaps for more personal reasons, we also have the rise of the 'gig economy'. There are industries where TCVs (temps, contractors and vendors) outnumber regular workers by 200%.[100] If a leader fails to provide an appropriate environment, this additional, attractive option to 'run free' is open.

Further, there is a current trend for many white-collar workers, disillusioned with corporate careers, to flee the office "to become brewers, bakers and pickle-makers".[101] Regardless of whether the trend is rational economic behaviour or the treacherous sexiness of entrepreneurship,[102] the impact is that employers 'compete' for labour not only with traditional competitors, but also with self-employment.

THE DISENGAGED WORKER

Let's say you get and keep your employee. Are they really productive?

Productivity is impacted by the employee's engagement. Apparently today's employee is fickle, and their engagement with business is potentially not high, at least according to the Gallup consultancy. Gallup says that we are in an "employee engagement crisis, with serious and potentially lasting repercussions for the global economy". Apparently only 32% of employees in the US are engaged, which compares favourably to their less engaged colleagues worldwide!

At just 13% engagement level worldwide, those workers must barely be present at all.[103]

Your role, as a leader, is to get the discretionary effort needed for the highest levels of performance. At the same time, as we have said, trust in management is at an all-time low.[104] Tough job you've got, eh?

THE LEADER'S PREDICAMENT

You are faced with a predicament.

On the one hand, the business environment is challenging. It is growing more complex, at an ever-increasing pace.

At the same time, the employees you rely on are more likely than ever to leave, including in order to work for a new, highly desirable boss – themselves. And, if they do elect to stay, they are likely to be disengaged. Employees want to grow but don't want to commit. And all of this impacts your results.

Concurrently, your job as a leader is changing. You have limited resources, a complex environment and seemingly conflicting demands, such as driving performance while keeping members of your team engaged.

So how do you get the best out of the people who work for you? You can, in a short space of time, improve the performance and productivity of your team in ways that can potentially engage them. The answer is simple. The answer is feedback.

And any leader can provide feedback. We all have the skills to execute this proven productivity-producing process.

So how are we doing?

As you know from the research we shared earlier, regardless of all the good reasons to do so, managers don't give feedback. TABLE 3 (next page) gives you a full list of the reasons, rationalizations and excuses that we consistently hear from managers around the world, across organizations. The predicament is universal, pervasive and deeply concerning.

TABLE 3: Reasons why managers don't give feedback

CATEGORY[105]	REASONS	WHAT THE MANAGERS THINK AND/OR SAY
NIL	• Lack of personal accountability	• "I don't do it because I don't have to (no leadership expectation or accountability)"
SKILL	• "I don't know how" • "I don't have the tools" • "I lack experience"	• "I am not trained to give feedback or I haven't done it before" • "I don't know the root cause of the problem" • "I know what needs to be said but I don't know how to say it" • "I don't do it frequently, so I am not good at it"
WILL …	**Rational thinking with skewed beliefs:** • Good intentions • Myths • Homegrown theories of performance • "There is no truth, anyway"	• "I don't have any answers – I don't know what they can do about it" • "I don't mind, so long as it is positive" • "I have to assess behaviours – that's 'personal'" • "It's pointless, people don't change anyway" • "I don't want to damage the relationship" • "It has to be balanced"

	Rational thinking with bad leadership:	• "I can't manage the employee's expectations"
	• Ill intent	• "The employee may leave! Or, at least, disengage"
	• Passive-aggressive	
	• Manipulative	• "The employee will go to Employee Relations, for sure"
	• "I'm afraid of accusation"	• "My opinion doesn't count anyway, so what's the point?"
	• "I don't want to be the bad guy"	• "My boss/others will just contradict me. I can't afford the merit/bonus budget to back up my positive feedback"
...	• Politics	
WILL	• Protecting your own turf	• "I'm not rewarded for it anyway"
		• "It takes too much time and I have to record it"
		• "I'll get a poor rating from my staff"
	Emotional:	• "It makes me feel awkward and vulnerable"
	• "It requires emotional resources"	• "The employee will disagree and it will result in an uncomfortable discussion"
	• "It causes stress and anxiety"	

KEY POINTS

The environment is difficult. You need to continually improve the performance of your employees, despite the increasing complexity and speed of the workplace. Your employees don't have to cooperate. They may be disenchanted with the organizational routines and, actually, have choices. We work in environments of low loyalty. Your leadership challenge is to boost performance in this environment. Feedback is an answer. Done properly, it increases performance and engagement.

EXPERT'S OPINION

IS FEEDBACK REALLY AN ANSWER?

Monika Hamori, professor, IE Business School
Monika is professor of human resources at IE Business School in Madrid. Monika is on the Thinkers50 Guru Radar and she has been honoured as one of the '40 Best Business School Professors Under 40'. Her research centres on organizational practices around managing and developing high-potential talent.

Today, more than ever, employees desire feedback from their superiors or from the people around them. The nature of work has changed dramatically in the past three decades and two of these important changes have increased employees' desire for feedback.

Change #1: Job security is on the decline and employees want to cash in

Traditionally, organizations in the developed world relied almost exclusively on skill development inside the organization. Companies hired employees at entry level, without experience, and developed their skills. The reward for good performance was promotion. Each promotion was preceded by training for the next job. Organizations provided job security and often lifetime employment in exchange for loyalty and adequate performance.

That traditional model has gone. Technological and economic changes have made some existing skills obsolete. Companies prefer to buy these skills in from the outside, or outsource these activities, rather than develop the skills internally.

With job security not a given, employees have two objectives when they join corporations: to cash in, or obtain the greatest immediate benefits from employers in terms of pay or promotions, and to increase their employability, as they constantly face the threat of having to find a new job. So, employees demand constant feedback on their performance: on how they are doing compared to peers, or on when the next promotion will come.

Change #2: Employers provide less and less support for employee development

In 2015 my co-author, Dr Jie Cao, and I conducted a global survey of graduates of a leading European business school to identify the development practices most effective in keeping young professionals at organizations.[106] We gave respondents a list of development practices. Since most managerial skills are acquired on the job, our list included several types of job-related experiences and other kinds of development: training, mentoring, coaching, support from senior management and the direct supervisor.

With respect to each of these practices, we asked our respondents two questions:

- How important is this practice to you?
- Does your employer provide you with this practice?

We drew two conclusions from this research. First, almost all of the 14 development practices were either very or extremely important to our respondents. Formal training, high-stakes jobs and support from senior management were the most important ones.

Second, when we looked at the gaps between the development practices our respondents considered important and those that they actually received from their employers, the gaps were relatively small with respect to on-the-job development practices.

However, the largest gaps existed between what respondents deemed important and what their jobs offered them with respect to mentoring and coaching, support from their direct manager and support from top management. These findings reveal that organizations – on average – provide much less interpersonal support than employees find important for their development.

Feedback is a way of closing this gap.

PART TWO

FairTalk Leader

Part One gave you knowledge about and principles of feedback. It was about what you need to know.

Part Two is all about the practicalities. We zoom right in to collecting the information, checking for accuracy and alignment, crafting a powerful message and delivering it successfully. In any situation. It is about what you do.

As such, this part of the book is at the heart of FairTalk, which is about giving feedback on things that matter, delivered in a way that enables high performance.

CHAPTER 6

Deciding 'What's Up?':
Diagnosing What Needs
to Be Improved

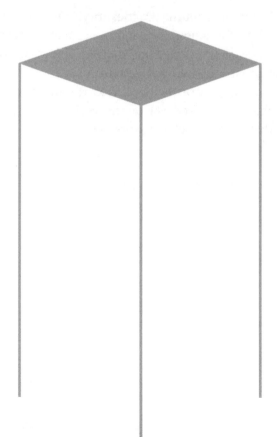

"A map is not functional until you know where you are on it."[107]

David Allen, productivity consultant

Most leaders know the areas in which their employees must improve. They know what they want to see. However, they may not be able to describe it in ways that are useful for improving performance.

This is typically not from a lack of innate ability. Anyone can do it. It does require time and attention to prepare.

But preparation does not have to be lengthy. All you need to do before you give FairTalk is to:

1. have a point of view about 'what matters' and describe what matters in terms of a learnable skill;
2. do an accuracy check;
3. validate your opinion, with input from others, before sharing.

For your convenience, FIGURE 8 gives you a map of this chapter:

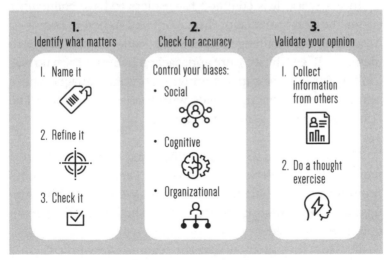

FIGURE 8: Preparing the FairTalk Statement

Let's start by figuring out what really matters.

IDENTIFY WHAT MATTERS

To make it simple – we are all about simplicity – we suggest that you start by naming the gap that, if filled, would lift performance.

So, let's start.

I. NAME IT

Describing the exact nature of an issue makes it real. Once it's real, it can be documented, examples can be given, and it can be measured and tracked. You can hold employees accountable. In TABLE I (page 39) we provided a list of competencies to help identify performance issues. It is a starting point. From there the question that moves the dialogue from the ideal thought, a complaint or a wish, to a performance improvement opportunity is "What is the observable behaviour I want to see"?

In our work, it is common for leaders to have complaints about the performance of direct reports. When it comes to describing the challenge, these same leaders can struggle to 'name it'. Recently, we were approached by a mentee who was looking for help to support a high-potential manager whose team was experiencing issues with work–life balance. The conversation went something like this.

Mentee: We need to do something about Robin (not his real name). He's too driven. It's an issue. There are complaints around work–life balance in his team. We need to give him feedback. Otherwise, his reputation as a high-potential person could be impacted.

Us: How do you know that the team is overworked?

Mentee: Everyone on the team is working long hours. There are continually late nights. Weekends... And, in one case, a New Year's Eve.

Us: Why does the team need to work late?

Mentee: You know what it is like. We set challenging deadlines.

Us: Why are the deadlines at risk?

Mentee: We have had some unfortunate circumstances that contributed to these delays.

Us: Were these foreseeable? Could he have anticipated these potential delays?

Mentee: Well, yes. Wait... Are you saying that Robin should have...?

What our mentee had named as 'too driven' was, on deeper reflection, an outcome of an observable behaviour: inadequate planning. This behaviour led to crises that sucked everybody in. Why does it matter? Because:

- better planning is a *learnable* skill;
- asking Robin to be 'less driven' may have reduced his performance while potentially not changing the work–life balance issues experienced by the team members;
- Robin's reputation for being too driven might have impacted his career while nobody addressed the root cause of him constantly being in fire-fighting mode.

A *FairTalk principle is focus*: expectations must be clear. If you can't name it, you can't reasonably expect someone else to fix it. *Focus* also means concentrating on only a few things – ideally one big, meaty developmental goal an employee can put all their energy into. This is what will best help them to perform at a higher level.

Another conversation we inevitably have with leaders is whether that area of focus should be on better leveraging strengths or overcoming weaknesses.

Our answer is both. You can further hone and perfect skills that have made you successful. At the same time, your weaknesses can get you into trouble. It is weaknesses that typically result in suboptimal performance. Nobody has been fired for doing good work, but many executives have failed because they ignored their weaknesses. Purely strength-based development is unfounded and can do more harm than good to performance and careers.[108]

Now, your team members may have never become great at their weakest competencies (sorry for the blunt truth!). But you can give feedback, and they can work on mitigating the impact.

So, name it.

2. REFINE IT

Once you have given something a name, it becomes real. It draws attention to something specific. Think about your right ankle. You see – before we called it out by its name, it was not in the field of your attention. Now you can scratch it, if you like. Specifics lead to action.

Of course, our conversation with our mentee about Robin did not end there. We took it further, refining 'driven for results' into 'planning', and then further into observable chunks – things like clear analysis of the external environment in order to anticipate obstacles, or estimating lead times, or monitoring progress against a project plan.

You can help your employees by breaking down big, fuzzy weaknesses into things you can see.

Even these chunks could be further refined. For example, is the project plan clearly understood by everyone on the team? If it isn't, that is a specific *something* an employee could work on.

The challenge is to focus on specifics rather than broad development needs. And our list in TABLE I (page 39) can help with that. The key is to find the *micro-skill* – the smallest possible unit of a learnable skill within a competency.

Development is most supported when we can identify these micro-skills and channel effort towards them.

3. CHECK IT

Now, check your choice.

Remember we defined our goal as naming the gap that needs filling and that, if filled, would lift performance.

Let's pause on that last phrase: 'would lift performance'.

All of us can do better. Probably across many things. But not everything will lift our performance. And certainly not everything will lift our performance equally. Your goal, as a leader, is to find the thing that, if addressed, would most impact the employee's success – or, more importantly, would best prepare them for their next challenge.

Which takes us back to the definition of FairTalk. FairTalk is feedback on things that matter, delivered in a way that will enable high performance. It is not about *everything* that can be done differently.

You now have a clear assumption about what needs to improve. It is clear, and it should actually help someone's development. But how accurate is your assumption?

CHECK FOR ACCURACY

It's time to talk about biases.

Our brain is fascinating. Weighing less than 2% of our body mass, it consumes more than 20% of our energy, and controls 1 billion neurons and a resulting 1 quadrillion synapses. (We didn't really count them.) In its most enlightened moments, it thinks it is rational, methodical and fair. The truth is that it is emotional, haphazard and biased. And we bring it to work every day. Yikes!

The brain has developed for efficiency, not effectiveness, and for fast, survival-essential decisions: is it safe or dangerous, are you friend or foe, do I belong or not? Asked to do more, it tires quickly, because it is wired for easy solutions. Therein lies the problem. Thinking requires energy. To conserve energy, the brain is attuned to provide easy solutions. To ensure that cognitive ease, it takes mental shortcuts and defaults to stereotypes, heuristics and rules of thumb... as well as the greatest mental shortcut of all – assumptions.

True to the above-average effect discussed in Chapter 3, research confirms that the majority of us believe that we are less biased than others. Adding insult to injury, we get defensive when factual feedback is provided demonstrating our biases.[109]

FIGURE 9: Organizational bias at work

There are many situations when biases and stereotypes serve us well. But these assumptions and biases also act as a filter. They impact our evaluations and distract from accuracy and consistency. Therefore, they have a limited place in accurate assessment and fair feedback.

TABLE 4 contains a list of common biases that directly impact the feedback process. While it is not exhaustive, it contains a lot. Identifying your bias correctly helps you to control it better.

TABLE 4: Biases in feedback: how biases impact our judgement

CATEGORY	TYPE OF BIAS	IMPACT ON FEEDBACK QUALITY
SOCIAL	**Similar-to-me bias (or affinity bias)** Tendency to give weight to things we personally value.	An example would be a leader who is highly conscientious and detailed. In looking to name what matters to performance, they may place a premium on the same personal discipline in others, while unconsciously discounting other skills, such as flexibility or agility.
	Strictness/ leniency bias Having different performance standards from others in the same organization.	Don't we all know of a manager who genuinely believes their team is the best? Conversely, we can always think of the managers who can't seem to be pleased. These are examples of the leniency and strictness biases, respectively. (Neither boss is ideal but, if you have to choose, take the lenient one!)
	Contrast bias Making swift judgements about someone based on a single comparison with a peer.	In order to decide 'what's up' quickly, an assessor with this bias looks for a contrast. For example, they might unconsciously compare others against the star performer, so that everyone fades in comparison. Or they might remember people who stand out more than others. An extroverted person may be better known but actually produce results of equal quality to someone else. *Conscious* comparison supports fairness. *Unconscious* comparison leads to a less-than-complete assessment of any gaps.

COGNITIVE ...	**Attribution error** Tendency to believe that people's behaviours reflect who they are.	When we think of ourselves, we tend to attribute positive outcomes to … ourselves. We ascribe success to our skills or experience, whereas we attribute negative outcomes to some other, external factor, such as bad luck. When we think of the performance of others, it's the opposite! We attribute their success to external factors (e.g. luck), while their failure to achieve certain objectives is supposedly due to their personal characteristics (e.g. laziness). When diagnosing 'what's up', this can be fatal.
	Confirmation bias A tendency for the brain to find evidence that supports an already held view while rejecting anything opposing it.	We tend not to seek information that might disprove what we believe. We 'find' examples and facts that support our already formed view of an employee's performance. And we unconsciously ignore evidence to the contrary.
	Overconfidence bias Being overly sure of our own abilities.	We believe that we are better judges of talent than we really are. Checking in with others and collecting various inputs on your employees' performance will help you keep your overconfidence under control.
	Inference bias Making connections where none exist.	Our brains like stories. We are wired to find coherence and links in our lives, even when there may be none. Daniel Kahneman calls this WYSIATI – What You See Is All There Is.[110] For example, you see an employee spending long hours at work. You decide that they are dedicated, going above and beyond. And it may be just that. Or they could be inefficient, taking longer than their colleagues to complete the same tasks. Or they could have personal problems and are avoiding going home. Why don't you ask and find out?

COGNITIVE ...	**Recency effect** A tendency to recall and weigh things that have happened most recently, ignoring prior events.	Good performers have bad days. Anyone can make a mistake. The fairness principle compels us to look over time when we are diagnosing 'what's up'. But our tired brain finds it easier to reach for the most recent examples.
	Halo and horns effects Tendency to let one positive or negative characteristic or event 'spill over' and influence how all other factors are assessed.	You may unwittingly turn a blind eye to many of an employee's transgressions because of something that they are brilliant at. This is a halo effect. You feel like you have taken an objective stance, but all your evidence is filtered through rose-coloured glasses created by one area of brilliance. The horns effect works in a similar way: just think of the case of an employee who messed up a project three years earlier and is still being punished for it.
	Negativity bias Tendency to assign greater importance and prominence to negative events, emotions and considerations.	Feedback has got its bad rap because it is often associated with something negative, and the negativity bias doesn't help. FairTalk requires a focus on things that matter, positive or negative. To be fair, you need to weigh both the good and the bad using the same measure.

ORGANIZATIONAL	Bandwagon bias Tendency to do what's trending: going along with the group's opinions or practices.	You won't be fair in your feedback if you just go along with what others say. If you are susceptible to the bandwagon bias, you may give greater value to the opinions of others and undervalue other data and facts, including your own observations.
	Deference bias (or authority bias) Giving greater weight to the opinions of superiors.	Some of us suffer from a natural, and unconscious, tendency to respect authority and hierarchy. We may overweigh the opinion of others, even when they have less data than we do. Your boss's perspective is important, but they may have a very specific and often narrow line of sight on your employee's performance. Form your point of view first (even better – write it down), and only then align it with that of your own manager.
	Reactance effect Unconscious urge to do the opposite of what others want, out of a need to resist attempts to constrain choice.	Ever found yourself disagreeing with someone without even being sure why? In discussing your team members' performance with your peers, for example, you may be tempted to argue the opposite case for an employee, merely out of the desire to push back against a contrary opinion. We don't like being told what to do.

You can use the table as a mental checklist to ensure that your assessment is fair and accurate.

VALIDATE YOUR OPINION

To make feedback fair and more credible, it is not enough to form your opinion and minimize the impact of your personal biases. You also need to seek varied inputs.

Why? Because your point of view depends only on your own perspective. And that is limited. Independent views of two or more people on someone else's performance are notoriously disparate. For example, in a study comparing performance ratings where there were two supervisors, there was only a 25% overlap.[111]

Further, evidence is consistent about the fact that individual evaluations of performance are frequently inaccurate and may lead to bad outcomes. Joint evaluations are fairer. It is fairness (much more than the actual outcome) that leads to employees owning results, accepting the corresponding feedback and being motivated to increase performance. And fairness leads to greater organizational performance.[112]

So, aligning your opinion about an employee's performance with the opinions of others is not only the right thing to do – it is also a smart thing to do.

Behavioural economics research tells us that people make more reasoned choices when examining options jointly rather than separately. Two studies demonstrate this point.

In one study, participants were asked to select a candidate for a job. They were given the results of the tests, mathematics and verbal, that the candidates had completed. In independent evaluations, participants were 16% more likely to choose a male over a female. What's worse, 62% of the participants chose a higher-performing candidate and 52% chose a lower-performing candidate – only a 10% difference! So performance hardly mattered.

However, in the same study, when there was joint evaluation, the likelihood that a lower-performing candidate was chosen was nearly zero. Higher-performing candidates were 46% more likely to be chosen compared to when evaluations were carried out independently, and the gender gap in selection had completely disappeared.[113] Yay!

In a different study, researchers demonstrated that, when we make decisions on our own, we are more affected by the negativity bias. We disproportionately take into account negative elements in our decision making. However, when we involve others in the process of evaluation, the balance between looking at the positives and negatives in performance outcomes is restored.[114]

Accuracy in evaluation leads to higher performance, and aligned views are more accurate. Therefore, aligning your point of view with that of others increases the fairness, focus and credibility of your feedback message.

There are two ways of gathering information in order to improve your accuracy. You can reach out to people who have a line of sight to your employee's performance or you can do a mental exercise comparing that performance against different parameters. We suggest that you do both.

I. COLLECT INFORMATION FROM OTHERS

We believe there are four sources of input you can consider.

Internal or external customers

Data is often collected from customers. They provide a legitimate, but limited, point of view. 'Limited' is the issue here. Customers' assessment is coloured by their unique position. Customers evaluate service levels, rather than performance, so opportunities for both accurate and fair assessment may be missed. Use this input, but weigh it appropriately. This avoids both over- and under-rating – for example, during extreme service conditions. It also ensures that your feedback doesn't reinforce the behaviour of employees who become simply 'yes men' or 'yes women' for the customer.

Stakeholders beyond customers

When we move from customers to stakeholders, we open the opportunity to collect data with the potential to be more rounded and therefore more developmental. In a matrixed organization (one where employees have dual reporting lines), there is no shortage of stakeholders who are not customers. An appropriate stakeholder can be a matrix partner. Make a list of a few key stakeholders for your employee. It does not need to be long, but it should be representative. While a customer is likely to be a good judge on the *what*, these non-customer stakeholders may be a good source of insights on the *how*.

Treat your boss as an independent source of data

Few managers provide feedback in a radically different way to their own boss's assessment. But *asking* your leader for insights can be valuable. Higher-level leaders have a broader business perspective, more points of comparison and are, quite literally, a step removed from your employee's work. This additional distance can be valuable. However, what your leader potentially doesn't have is the ability to observe the employee in action, so, as in all sources of assessment, weighing the employee's contribution is the key.

Alternatively, you can try to put yourself in the shoes of your boss and answer these questions:

- What does your employee's performance look like from their position?
- How do your empolyees compare in terms of their performance with the employees of your peers?
- What opportunities has your boss had to observe your employees perform? How did they do?

Of course, imagining your boss's thinking process is a valuable exercise in distancing yourself and being more strategic in your own evaluation. But the best way of getting their point of view is to ask. Think of two or three questions you would pose to your boss to gain a better perspective on your employees' performance.

Employee's own view

You can consider asking the employee themselves to provide a summary of their accomplishments and examples of their behaviour. There are many issues with self-assessment. One is the bias created by the above-average effect (discussed in Chapter 3). It is very likely that the employee will have a high opinion of their own performance. Another issue with self-assessment is that people assign the greatest value to the effort they have put into a task, with a lesser regard to the outcome. This should not be acceptable in a high-performing company that values impact, not only effort.

Conversely, asking your employees for a self-assessment can lead to greater engagement, ownership of the outcomes and motivation to develop further. But you need to be prepared to manage any potential discrepancy between your own view and that of your employee.

We invite you to reflect on two questions before you decide to invite your employees to provide opinions on their own performance:

- How much value will it add – to you and your employees – to invite the employee to self-assess?
- How will you position this exercise to the employee?

2. DO A THOUGHT EXERCISE

There are other ways of checking your feedback message for accuracy. If you cannot get a second opinion on your employee's performance, you can consider a few factors to compare it against.

Comparisons with the natural peer group

Where possible, peer-to-peer comparison provides a good calibration of performance, especially on technical or functional performance. However, in comparing peers in similar roles, remember the goal is not to compare styles. Focus on achieving the goals as well as the corresponding behaviours that either help them or hinder their success.

Consider your employee's goal attainment and behaviours over the past quarter, six months or twelve months. How does it compare to that of their peers? Thinking this through will give you an idea as to whether the employee is superior, inferior or on par with their peers with regard to achieving goals and demonstrating expected behaviours.

Move beyond those in similar roles

A traditional approach to diagnosing performance gaps usually includes comparisons with peers in similar roles, as outlined above. But, for a richer understanding, consider looking at peers in very different roles. This can provide helpful insights, because it can allow for comparisons against the best in class. While the technical skills differ, you can draw valid comparisons on leadership or managerial skills. You can compare strategic thinking, or project management, or team leadership, or presentation skills, or anything else. And doing this also raises standards. You are no longer assessing the best leaders among engineers, but the best leaders. Suddenly, the insights you collect increase dramatically.

Contrast against the employee's previous year of performance

Every year is different and performance changes over time. But radical changes in performance raise flags. If a traditionally strong performance is followed by a poor result, your assessment could be valid. However, ask yourself, "Did one issue or error inappropriately colour my overall assessment?" Watch out for the halo and horns effects (see TABLE 4 on page 93)! And keep in mind that the reverse situation holds true too. When a typically lower performer puts in a great year, it is fair to ask yourself whether you are evaluating their actual results or responding to the change. If your interest is an accurate diagnosis, compare against the employee's history – not to have history determine your view but rather to ask insight-seeking questions.

Compare against industry standards or norms
While we tend to make comparisons internally to diagnose performance gaps, as a leader you will also have contrast points from a broader experience. It is appropriate to consider how an employee compares to external talent performing in similar roles. This may be difficult to do in some cases, but the best leaders can give developmental feedback not only on how their employees perform internally but also on how their employees compare to the 'best of the best'. How? It may be easier than you think. Consider these questions:

- Based on your knowledge of the market, how easy would it be to replace this employee with someone who would perform at the same or a higher level?
- In interviews with external candidates at a similar level, has there been someone who utterly impressed you?
- When you speak with your counterparts from other companies, how do they describe the level of performance outcomes of their team members?

The more you train your eye to spot talent both internally and externally, the easier it will be for you to compare your team members against industry standards and, in so doing, more accurately diagnose performance opportunities.

Against the levels above and below

Finally, we find it helpful to compare employees with the levels above and below. Are they close to senior colleagues with respect to their skills? Which skills? This is automatically a source of rich feedback on their strengths. If they have gaps in comparison with the next level that can be isolated, you have a great source of developmental feedback. Similarly, when you compare them with those in lower grades. If an employee is not significantly advanced compared to more junior staff, you should ask yourself in what way this is so. This will give you insight into where the employee has scope to improve.

FROM COLLECTING DATA TO GIVING FAIRTALK FEEDBACK

How do these exercises help you improve feedback accuracy? By forcing you to engage your conscious mind, they make you override the default that otherwise lets assumptions, bias and shortcuts take over. You can make the unconscious conscious.

Bringing it all together, FIGURE 10 (next page) depicts these various sources of insight.

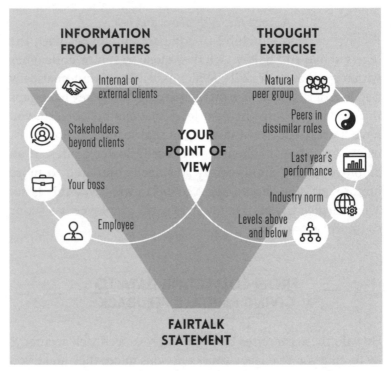

FIGURE 10: Sources of information that can be used to align your feedback message

With this information you now have all you need to diagnose your employees' performance.

It does take some time and effort to do this for each of your employees – time that is always scarce. You should certainly do this when you just joined the team and need to have an informed view.

The rest of the time, you may want to focus on your most critical team members, or those most in need of focused development.

You are now in a position to give fair, focused and credible feedback. And in the next chapter you will learn a simple yet powerful formula to help you craft your feedback message.

KEY POINTS

To give feedback, leaders need to have a point of view about 'what matters'. The competency list provided in Chapter 2 (see TABLE 1 on page 39) helps you to name the gap. Helpful feedback describes what matters in terms of a learnable skill. The discipline of subjecting your diagnosis of an issue to the inputs of others leads to more accurate assessment and, consequently, better feedback and performance. It also checks for unconscious bias.

EXPERT'S OPINION

USEFUL FEEDBACK GOES BEYOND
STRENGTHS AND WEAKNESSES

> Rob Kaiser, president, Kaiser Leadership Solutions
> Rob is a thought leader, adviser and consultant on the subject of leadership. His articles in journals such as *Harvard Business Review* and *MIT Sloan Management Review*, as well as his books *Filling the Leadership Pipeline*, *The Versatile Leader* and *The Perils of Accentuating the Positive*,[115] provide simple yet comprehensive advice on building stronger leadership.

Let's face it: giving direct, candid feedback isn't easy. It's hard to land a compliment about what an employee does well, and even harder still to find the right time, tone and words to let them know what needs improvement. But the essential task of providing useful performance feedback is made more complicated by the oversimplified way most of us think about performance.

The default mindset is defined by the simple dichotomy of strengths and weaknesses: what someone does well is a strength, and what they don't do very well is a weakness. Cut and dried. Case closed.

It turns out that performance isn't so simple. A game-changing insight from a study at the Center for Creative Leadership – an insight obscured by the recent fad of focusing on strengths – is that executives rarely fail because of weaknesses. Actually, it's hard to ascend to a leadership role without a lot of strengths and few glaring weaknesses. Ironically, failure is often the result of strengths that become weaknesses through overuse: technical expertise becomes tunnel vision, drive and ambition become abrasiveness, and even participation can devolve into ineffectual overinclusion.

An effective way to give feedback that is easier to receive and, not coincidentally, more helpful is based on a three-category scheme that separates what a person does *too little* from what they do *too much* and, like Goldilocks' porridge, distinguishes these from what the individual does *just right*.

Making room for overused strengths makes possible a new type of conversation, one that affirms what a person has going for them while also giving them a chance to get better and become more effective. People don't overdo things on purpose – they are usually trying their best to get a certain result but aren't thinking about unintended consequences. For instance, the eager beaver is quick to speak up with good ideas in a meeting – but doesn't realize how this crowds others out.

This sets up a conversation about the possibility of there being too much of a good thing as well as complementary skills and behaviours that may need to be built up. Consider the analogy of a volume control – dialling up or dialling down as the situation requires.

Of course not every performance issue is a matter of strengths being overused. Sometimes it is a simple lack of skill or know-how. But test the idea out: reframe the issue and see whether you can draw a connection to something the person is actually pretty good at, but perhaps takes too far and at the expense of a complementary skill or behaviour that could also be helpful. Talking from this perspective can help team members become more well-rounded employees who can make the most of their strengths – without going overboard.

CHAPTER 7

The Three Steps to
Powerful Feedback

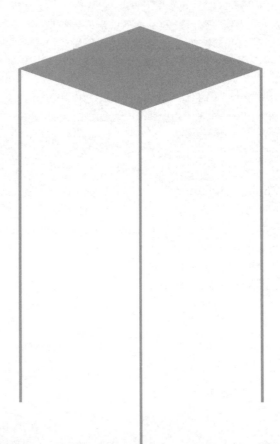

"Most great leaders use a feedback model, one they have mastered to the point that it is constantly in play during the conversation but invisible to the receiver."[116]

Jay Zimmerman, talent leader, Aon

In Chapter 5 we described today's complex world of work: a blurred line of sight to knowledge work and workers, increased pressure from an erratic external environment, and a new deal with workers in which engagement, commitment to a single employer and even the desire to be an employee differ radically from the past.

Increasing performance in this environment is vital. And evidence confirms that good feedback achieves this; given timely and specific feedback, humans give tasks a greater share of attention, dedicate more time and expend greater effort.[117]

Yet, managers don't tend to give performance feedback. As we have said, it is too difficult, too scary or just 'not my job'. So we have to make it simple.

Here are three easy steps for giving highly effective feedback.[118]

STEP 1: "TELL ME WHY IT MATTERS"

A Harvard psychologist, Ellen Langer, conducted a famous experiment in the 1970s to identify the power of *why*. Researchers approached 120 people waiting in line to make copies at the City University of New York library. They asked either for a small favour (to copy five pages) or a big favour (to copy 20 pages). They gave one of three types of explanation:

1. **They gave no explanation.** "Excuse me, I have five (or 20) pages. May I use the Xerox machine?"

2. **They gave placebic information.** "Excuse me, I have five (or 20) pages. May I use the Xerox machine, because I have to make copies?"

3. **They gave real information.** "Excuse me, I have five (or 20) pages. May I use the Xerox machine, because I'm in a rush?"

Langer discovered that, for a small favour, even a request without explanation was granted in 60% of cases. When placebic information was provided, 93% of people let the person cut in front. Providing the full, real information increased that number to 94%.

However, for a big favour – copying 20 pages – the situation was very different. With a request only, or a request with a placebic explanation, people agreed in only 24% of cases. Importantly, when people were given real information, with a sufficient reason, the number almost doubled, increasing to 42%.[119]

How does this relate to performance and feedback? Merely telling people that they need to change is not enough. If the adjustment in behaviour is small, a superficial explanation may suffice. However, if you want to see meaningful change (probably in the majority of cases), you need to explain *why* the change is important and how it will impact performance.

While the science confirms the power of *why*, this also makes sense intuitively. If you believe that people are generally rational, prefer to do a good job rather than a poor one and prefer to get along with others, then you will believe that they would try to change provided there is a good reason. Kate Sweetman, a leadership expert, affirms that it's your role to make that link to results clear:

When making the case for change, the leader must clearly show the likely future if we stay the same, and equally clearly show the likely future if we make the changes proposed. The perceived benefits of change must be significantly greater than the perceived cost of staying as we are.[120]

There is another, more pragmatic consideration. If something is important enough to be worthy of feedback, you should be able to articulate why it matters. If you can't say why a topic is worth attention, maybe it is not worthy of feedback. It will just muddy the waters.

So, start with why it matters.

Let's imagine an employee and how you could begin FairTalk with her:

Sam, collaboration between marketing and sales determines speed to market. It is especially important for success in brand management. The way you interact with your colleagues impacts how soon new products hit the shelves.

This is a neutral but powerful statement. You haven't given any feedback yet but you have already established the importance of collaboration in the context of the *results*, and the requirements for success. These words also signal that this is important to you.

By connecting your feedback to the *why* – that is, the purpose or meaning – you:

I. **Frame**. The feedback is now about 'it' (collaboration) and not about 'them'(personal). You increase the chance the recipient will actually listen. Connecting to this bigger why appeals to those who care about outcomes. And to those who value the big picture. And those who respond to leader expectations. Konstantin Korotov, ESMT professor, told us that:

   This approach works even for those who are patholog-ically unable to hear feedback. For example, those with big egos or little concern for others. They care about being successful. Framing the feedback as a means to achieving their personal objectives will get you further than appealing to what is good or what is right.[121]

2. **Link**. You have also created the link between *their* behaviour and *their* success. Once something is personally important, people are motivated to change.[122] Linking behaviours with attaining organizational goals increases motivation and clarifies the company's expectations. This approach works.[123]

3. **Begin**. Okay, it's now 'out there'. Often the hardest thing to do in giving feedback is to start. Even if all else fails, you've started.

You have now identified a specific behaviour that connects to results. And feedback needs to be like a rifle shot, remember? You have focused only on what matters. And said why. It is clear and unequivocal. Don't pile on.

Too much feedback can be counterproductive.[124] If you keep listing problems, you risk demotivating others. You risk being a nag, a micro-manager, fastidious or unrealistic. When a leader can zoom in on what is critical and state why the subject of the feedback matters to organizational outcomes, they are simply more likely to get better results.

The first question in the FairTalk Statement: "Why does it matter?" It prompts you to take into account those on both sides of the table. Where can you connect the feedback to the receiver's desires as a professional and as a person? And why does this feedback matter to you? This first question also turns your mind to the organization as a stakeholder that needs to be satisfied. So, in the span of a few minutes, the model has helped you to be ready.[125]

STEP 2: "TELL ME HOW I'M DOING"

Okay, so we've established that something is sufficiently important for your employee to keep listening, so now it's time to talk about how things are going.

Regardless of your company's rating scale, definitions or guidelines around performance management, looking back at how someone has performed always starts with a simple question: "Did the employee meet expectations, exceed them or fall short?"

"Tell me how I'm doing" steers you straight to the thing you need to manage – the feedback itself:

Sam, your level of collaboration with sales falls short of expectations, especially around brand plans.

or

Sam, you aren't meeting expectations around collaboration as it relates to keeping sales informed about changes to brand plans.

Feels uncomfortable? Maybe. But look what just happened.

The employee knows their performance didn't meet standards or that they can be even greater at what they do. It is clear and unequivocal.

And even a vague notion, such as collaboration, becomes specific enough to be something someone can address.

And now, before you elaborate, explain, provide examples, justify the reasons or, worse, start to sugar-coat – *stop*.

You did it!

And, if you stayed true to the foundational principles that lead to feedback being effective (Chapter 4), your feedback will have been:

I. **Fair.** You have been honest and transparent. People want to know where they stand. They want to know "how I'm doing".

2. **Focused**. You have identified the behaviour, in this example collaboration, without cluttering it with too many details. You have also presented it in such a way that the employee cannot easily say, "But I didn't know."

3. **Credible**. Defensiveness stops a lot of important feedback ever being heard.[126] Even when it is delivered well. Credibility comes from you, from the message itself or from both. Even if the employee stops listening at this point, next time you can build on the fact that they know exactly where they stand.

If you only did this much, as a leader, you would already be well ahead of most.

But you can achieve even more!

STEP 3: "TELL ME WHAT TO DO"

Your role as manager isn't to persuade beyond a point but to communicate expectations and tell people how to meet the expectations.[127]

At this point, you need to recognize, reinforce or reward good behaviours, or alternatively ask for improvement.

The third part of the FairTalk Statement is about expectations.

When it comes to the "Tell me what to do" part of the FairTalk Statement, we like the word 'expectation'. Compare this with "It would be good if you..." Is this a request or a suggestion? Don't leave it to chance.

Also, compare the phrase "I expect you to..." with "I need you to..." The second phrase sounds like you don't personally want it, but you need it. By using this phrase, you distance yourself from accountability. It's almost apologetic.

Don't apologize. You are the leader. You have the right, we would even say the obligation, to set expectations.

"I expect you to…" is a powerful way to set the performance standard for your employee:

Sam, going forward, I expect you to learn the skill of keeping others informed by consistently sharing information and doing so proactively. This ensures sales have timely information, can take decisions quickly and get products on shelves sooner.

In this final step it is important that the feedback language is:
1. detailed;
2. destination focused;
3. doable;
4. developmental.

We'll explore each of these in turn.

DETAILED

Ah, those micro-skills we talked about. In the example of Sam, where the focus of the performance improvement is on 'informing others', you have provided a clear expectation for the employee. You have left no doubt about the behaviour you expect to see. But, importantly, you have also left a mile of room for the employee to decide *how* they will do that.

Sam might decide to hold monthly conference calls to share updates. She could elect to start a newsletter for the sales team. She could spend more time with regional sales managers. Go Sam!

And Sam's efforts will be directed correctly. Provided that an employee hears the feedback and is resolved to act upon it, they have two possible strategies: working harder or working smarter. When feedback contains specific indications of what needs to be changed ("Sam, you aren't sharing information on brand plans"), the recipient is more likely to work smarter.[128] When the message contains no such information ("Sam, build bridges with sales"), people are likely to invest more time and energy in the less effective ways that they have been relying on to date.

Providing specifics also leads to greater feedback acceptance. In a series of three experiments, researchers proved that logically taking people step by step through the feedback message helped them to remove any defensive barriers.[129]

DESTINATION FOCUSED

Marshall Goldsmith has written extensively on how applying a future focus changes receptivity to feedback.[130] While you cannot change the past, you can influence the future. Telling people what you expect them to learn or do differently is actionable, future focused and non-threatening. You are no longer discussing the mistakes of the past but, instead, examining opportunities to be great in the future.

DOABLE

If you have used the FairTalk diagnostic approach, you have already assessed that the development is feasible. You will have taken stock of the 3 Cs (capabilities, characteristics and context) to establish that the change is possible. And you have mentally checked your expectations against yardsticks, such as people in similar roles (Chapter 6).

It is important for your expectation to be 'doable'. An achievable expectation motivates and makes the employees believe in themselves. Yes, your goal is to increase performance. But it is effective to frame your feedback as an achievable learning goal. This approach positively impacts the level of effort, the nature and the extent of the goal, and self-efficacy of the individual.

In a study, a group of students were given a challenging task. They received feedback on how well they performed. Some received feedback in the form of a learning goal. Others received feedback with a 'proving orientation' –

that is, feedback asking them to better prove their own skills to themselves and/or others next time. Then the students were given a new, challenging task. Those who had been given a learning goal outperformed the others on the second task.[131] That is, those motivated to change through personal growth outperformed those trying to prove themselves.

DEVELOPMENTAL

Curiously, one of the best ways to attack a problem is to not focus on feedback directly. Instead, put the emphasis on learning and continuously improving business outcomes.[132]

You can use the FairTalk Statement in various ways. Sam's example above might be heard during a one-to-one or in a year-end review of goals. But the same simple FairTalk Statement works equally well for providing in-the-moment feedback.

Scientists have found that people are much more likely to act on feedback when the performance ("Tell me how I'm doing") and development ("Tell me what to do") discussions take place at the same time. Say why it's important and direct the action. When the development conversation is separated from the performance conversation, we are less motivated to change.[133] People must understand why they need to act on their development.

We have established that we may not like feedback but we must be satisfied with it. Adding the developmental piece can do just that. When your teams receive the feedback they need, act on it, see the results and learn – sure, they'll want more of that. Yes, in this way you can make them feedback junkies! Being repeat customers for feedback will unlock other related performance drivers: *feedback utility* (it helps them achieve their goals), *accountability* (they will do their jobs well), *self-efficacy* (they will be able to perform their tasks) and *social awareness* (they will take others' opinions of their work seriously).[134]

FROM FEEDBACK TO COACHING

If you deliver nothing more than the FairTalk Statement, you have provided a compelling reason to care, given accurate feedback against your expectations, and made a clear behavioural statement of what learning you expect in the future.

We love feedback. We believe most people want to do the right thing. They may lack awareness on how they are behaving today. They may underestimate the importance of the right behaviour in their performance. They may not be clear on what you wanted to see done differently. But feedback can give them this missing information.

It is acceptable to give feedback with a clear expectation of change and allow a mature person to work on realizing that change.

Actually, you may prefer to leave things that way. Research shows that unfinished business is remembered better. The Zeigarnik effect, named after the Russian-born psychologist Bluma Zeigarnik, means that things left unfinished, conversations without a closure and problems without a solution stay in our minds longer.[135] If you leave your feedback after the three-part statement ("Tell me why it matters," "Tell me how I'm doing" and "Tell me what to do"), you provide your employees with room to think about how they can improve.

But, if you want to go further, the FairTalk Statement is a powerful stepping stone towards quality coaching.

After the three-part feedback statement, asking a strong question (e.g. "When could you demonstrate this new behaviour?") instantly and seamlessly turns the feedback conversation into a coaching conversation.

We have six powerful coaching questions, designed to help you move from feedback to coaching. Questions for daily coaching that can seamlessly follow a FairTalk Statement include:

1. What options for action can you take?
2. Of these options, which one will you start with?
3. Is there anything preventing you from moving forward?
4. Who might be able to help you?
5. How will I and others know that you are making progress?
6. When will we get together to discuss how you are improving?

We like these questions a lot.

We don't like coaching questions that open a discussion about whether or not the feedback is accurate or legitimate.

Exploring the current state or how others see things may help, but in our view these discussions are better suited to longer-term coaching assignments. In-the-moment coaching is just that – it needs to move to action quickly.

By the way, if you want to be great at coaching, you can also add a vote of confidence in the employee, if you believe it, or add additional motivation, by simply reinforcing 'why it matters'.

TRACKING PROGRESS

One of the above powerful coaching questions addresses the idea of how employees will know they are making progress. Having them contemplate this is helpful. But the best, most accurate source to assess their progress is you, their leader!

Whether it takes the form of in-the-moment feedback or feedback associated with more formal evaluation, tracking progress is critically helpful. It is helpful if the employee improves their performance as you can use it to reinforce their positive development. Or, if the employee is not improving their performance, it can be used as a set of expectations. By tracking progress, you have a basis on which to give additional feedback, along the lines that your expectations have still not been met.

How will you look for evidence of progress? Based on your feedback, identify what might be considered 'moments of demonstration'. Where would you expect to see change? Start by looking there, for big and small improvements.

If you are not in a position to observe, you can also collect feedback from others.

Plan to track progress, recognize progress and reward success.

PULLING THE FAIRTALK MODEL TOGETHER

The FairTalk model (FIGURE II on page 122) is a systematic approach to successfully diagnosing and communicating performance gaps. The FairTalk Statement communicates the feedback in a clear and compelling way. And the fact that it is a model doesn't mean it needs to be formulaic:

About ten years ago the industry was driven by a formulaic approach. For any need there was a feedback formula. Now people want less of that. Today the trend is towards giving principles and coaching the leaders on how to apply them. It is about learning by doing. Now it's about wanting more simplicity, key themes and practice.[136]

The FairTalk model is simple and structured. You may wonder whether that structure would make it mechanical. It's a fair concern.

Jay Zimmerman upholds the value of a feedback model for the practising leader:

How do they follow the model without shuffling papers or sounding like a corporate robot? The answer lies in using the model as a tool to conduct the conversation but also to organize thoughts and devise a game plan. As the conversation takes its turns, the model guides you to a safe place and provides a path back when you are ready to return. Although you represent the organization and control the feedback, the model protects your precious connection to the receiver and helps them hear the message you are there to deliver.[137]

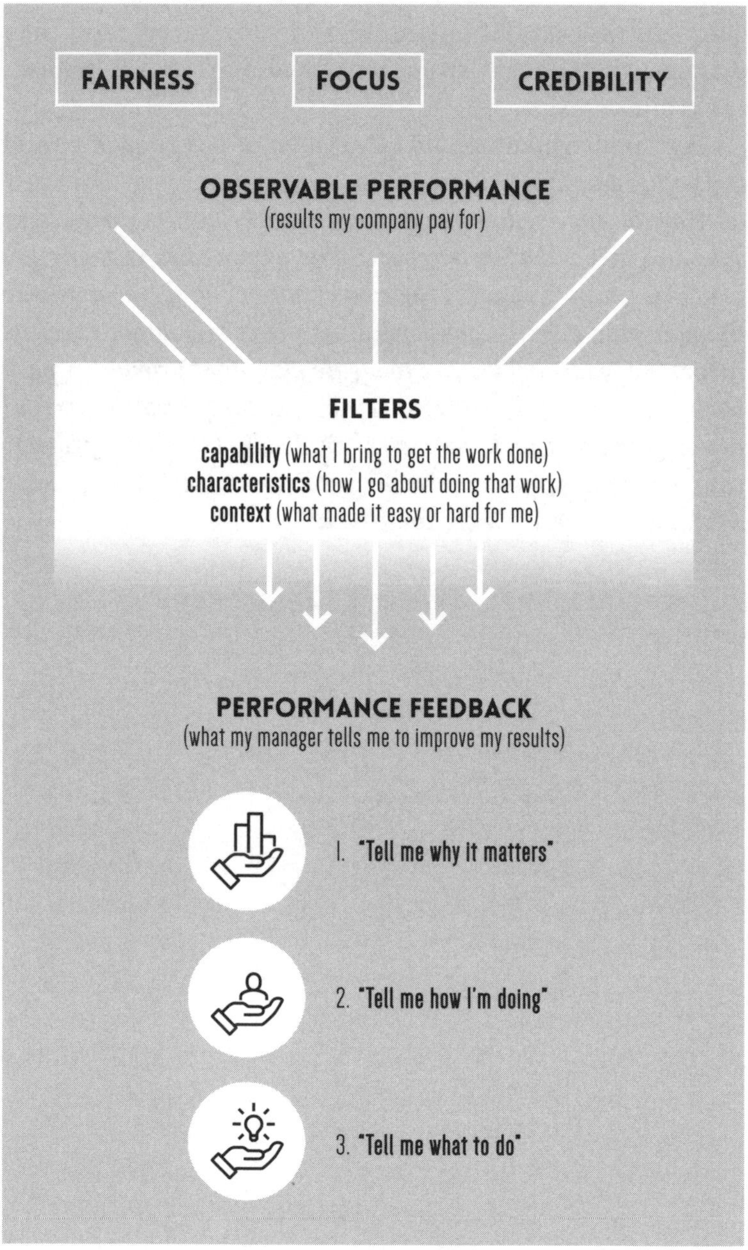

FIGURE II: The FairTalk model

KEY POINTS

A simple three-part FairTalk Statement can provide feedback in ways that align to well-researched, proven and effective methods. It provides employees with a fair, focused and credible assessment; clear expectations for the future; and a developmental 'blueprint'. Following the FairTalk Statement with action-oriented questions transforms feedback delivery into coaching.

EXPERT'S OPINION

THE ROLE OF A FEEDBACK MODEL

Jay Zimmerman, talent leader, Aon
Jay is the global talent leader for Aon's retirement, investment and talent consulting businesses. He previously worked as a consultant at Korn Ferry, advising clients on their human capital and specializing in leadership assessment.

"That's it?" asked the candidate. I scanned his assessment report. "Yes. Yes, it is," I replied. Long silence. "Seems like a lot to go through for that." He wasn't wrong, having endured a six-hour assessment of his personality, cognitive ability, experience and leadership. In nearly all aspects, he had been found wanting. I glanced over the feedback model and the script for unsuccessful candidates. It did not really matter, as we were already past our allotted half-hour.

The candidate and several other unfortunates were among the first people I gave feedback to during my ten years as an assessment specialist. In those early days, I only saw two people in the room:

1. **myself** and
2. **the feedback receiver**.

With practice, I realized three other invisible yet pivotal entities also have a seat in every feedback conversation:

3. **Desire**. Both the giver and the receiver bring desires both as professionals and as vulnerable, messy humans with hopes, fears and every other emotion. Sometimes the two are at cross-purposes.

4. **The organization**. More than just a logo, the organization is often the most powerful entity in the room – especially if most of the feedback is negative or the receiver's job may soon be in jeopardy. You both work for the organization but, in the feedback dynamic, the giver acts as its representative. This power-position can push the receiver to the outside, which is a lonely, scary place to be.
5. **Feedback itself**. In the receiver's mind, the feedback is like a mysterious animal in a cage under a black cloth. What does it look like? Will it bite? Who will look after it once this meeting is over? Even if you smile as you set the cage on the table, the receiver's defences are up until they see whether it's a rabbit or a rattlesnake.

Perceiving these three extra entities was a turning point in my maturation as a feedback giver. How could I say what must be said, portray the feedback accurately, do what the company requires *and* do right by the person across the table? What got me there was a simple, flexible feedback model such as the one you learned in this chapter. It is indispensable to anyone who accepts the complex responsibility of evaluating another human being and telling them about it to their face.

Mastery of the model will help *you* recognize when to move away from the *feedback*, set aside the demands of the *organization* and refocus on the *desires* of the *receiver*. Think of it as five acquaintances engaged in conversation at a cocktail party. You recognize when Receiver is feeling distressed and you gracefully ask Organization and Feedback, "Could you two please give us a moment alone?"

There are successful managers who find models formulaic and constraining. Their preference is to shoot from the hip. It is a rare breed who can do this and not leave a little blood on the floor. In my experience, this is often a sign of low self-awareness or even managerial laziness. Good leaders strategize on feedback, practise it and reflect on it afterward.

CHAPTER 8

Trap I: Competence.
Why Do I Get It Wrong?

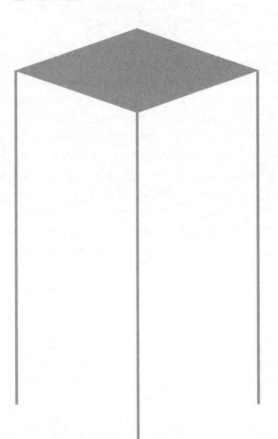

"Most of the evil in this world is done by people with good intentions."[138]

T.S. Eliot, Nobel Prize-winning poet

Remember we shared that only about half of feedback interventions result in greater productivity?[139] In other words, the other half doesn't! Well, done wrongly, in one third of cases, performance actually decreases after feedback.[140] As leaders, we haven't yet successfully cracked the code on how to give feedback that drives improved performance.

So, feedback can be ineffective. There are three types of ineffective feedback. A simple way to remember this is to think of the 3 Bs:

- **Baffling**. Feedback is baffling if the receiver does not know what to do with it. The message may be clear, but it is not actionable or is even completely irrelevant.
- **Bogus**. You might be tempted to alter the feedback message to one that is easier to give but is not entirely true. Bogus feedback is feedback that is inaccurate or manipulated (consciously or unconsciously).
- **Brutal**. Some things are best left unsaid. Even though they are true, communicating them might do more harm than good. And often the style (how) can wound more than the message (what).

We will look at each of these three in detail. FIGURE 12 (next page) contains a roadmap for you to follow through.

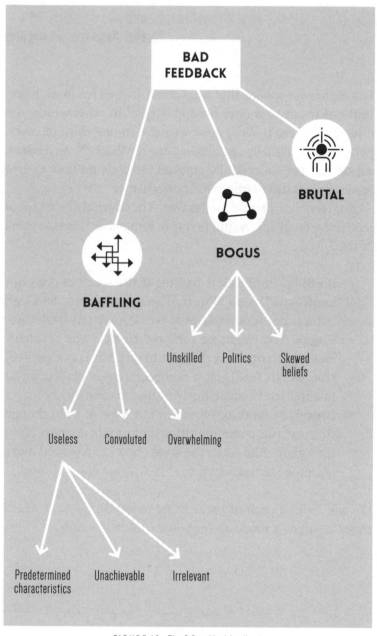

FIGURE 12: The 3 Bs of bad feedback

BAFFLING FEEDBACK

Baffling feedback is feedback the receiver can't do anything with.

Have you ever been lost even when you have a map? Or facing a 'do not enter' sign while your GPS tells you to proceed? Or following directions that are out of date and where the streets are no longer the same? Some forms of feedback can produce the same effect. While it may appear reasonable on the surface, it actually confuses. Then frustrates. And ultimately demotivates more than informs or energizes. You feel lost.

With baffling feedback, the message may be clear (proceed straight ahead) but it is not actionable (do not enter) or is completely irrelevant (there's no longer any street!).

As practitioners, we see many examples of baffling feedback. Here are the three we observe most frequently: useless, convoluted and overwhelming. Let's look at each of these separately.

USELESS

Don't give feedback that's useless. It's... useless!

> *If you don't believe the individual can or should make the expected changes, consider whether the feedback may be gratuitous, and thus not worth giving.*[141]

Following are three examples of such feedback.

Feedback on predetermined characteristics

Telling someone they need to be 'smarter' is a form of useless feedback. It is likely to lead to frustration. Intelligence is one example of a predetermined characteristic. It is fixed sometime after adolescence[142] and there is little that the employee or the employer can do to increase IQ. You may as well ask someone to "be taller".

Instead, it is much more useful to give feedback on a person's thought process or their information-processing skills, such as "The framework you used for the analysis isn't appropriate" or "You spend too much time summarizing the data." In these instances, your role is to refocus the feedback on the things that can change. If you identify specific actions that someone can take, they can still improve their performance.

Feedback that's unachievable

Each of us has a limit. Despite the claims of some self-development literature, our potential is real, measurable and finite.[143] Some of us may have huge potential and can be challenged to grow exponentially. But, for most people, you need to focus feedback on growth that is smaller and more achievable. Challenging an expert administrator with only average potential to "be more strategic" is unlikely to produce meaningful results. Focus on something closer to the task at hand, such as "I would like to see you work on setting goals for the following year and creating a plan for execution." The expert administrator will absolutely be able to craft and adhere to a plan. In this instance, the plan will be anchored in a (slightly) longer-term vision (goal) with a road map to get there (strategy). Go for targets that match the employee's growth potential. This will help them to improve their performance while potentially increasing their motivation. The alternative sets both sides up for failure.

Feedback that's irrelevant

Feedback can be delivered on anything. Is that feedback meaningful? Will it move the needle on performance? How is it useful for personal growth and career development? We can all get better at something. But this 'something' must be directly relevant to what we do today or something that we will be doing in the future. If you give unrelated feedback, you have already missed a valuable opportunity to deliver a performance-enhancing message that really matters. Did you know that humour is a competency? It is.[144] You could give feedback to an employee on the need to increase their humour. But what are the chances that displaying more humour will drive better business results?[145] Maybe not much, unless of course the job is clown!

CONVOLUTED

Convoluted means scrambled. It means overcomplicated. It means "I can't make head or tail of this." While simplicity makes feedback impactful, we are trained to make things more complex. At school, you get a higher grade when you use a more learned word or a compound sentence. But focus is one of the fundamental principles of good feedback. So keep it simple!

Simple doesn't mean incomplete. Employees do appreciate the background information on the order of priority and the bigger *why*,[146] and it's the first piece of your three-part FairTalk Statement. It can be included as long as it doesn't steal the focus from the feedback itself – that is, the assessment of current performance against expectations, and the call to action.

We typed 'confusing speeches' into a browser search field and got hundreds of pages and videos with splendid examples of what a straightforward message should *not* be. Try it.

The opposite of convoluted is plain, straightforward, pithy, concise – pick your favourite adjective. It can be difficult to sum up thoughtful observations and a range of inputs into a few pithy statements. Difficult, but not impossible. The FairTalk Statement makes complex information about your employees' performance simple and useful.

OVERWHELMING

What makes someone overwhelmed?

A computer freezes either when there are too many programmes running at the same time or when the single task that it is working on requires gigantic computational power. Just like when your computer freezes, our brain capacity has limits. Our ability to process feedback is a matter of timing and/or quantity.

Have you heard the common advice about giving feedback as soon after the observed instance as possible? Well, there is a caveat there. Check first whether the employee can make space to take in your message. Maybe emotions are still high. Or maybe there are two more meetings coming up and they need to prepare. Getting the timing wrong can make your feedback feel overwhelming.

The same goes for quantity. One common criticism of annual performance reviews is that managers try to fit in all the feedback they have collected over the year into a one-hour meeting. It's just too much.

We hear similar views from people who go through their first comprehensive assessment. They are overwhelmed by the sheer amount of information being thrown at them. A skilled coach can distil that complexity into a few relevant themes, something digestible and actionable. This is what you, as a leader, must do with feedback. Think back to our analogy of a funnel (see FIGURE 6 in Chapter 2). There will never be a shortage of data. But there may be a shortage of attention and the capacity to focus on what's essential.

We often observe leaders giving baffling feedback early in their careers. Yet this behaviour is easily corrected with training and practice. Even by reading this book, you are already reflecting on the utility of the feedback that you give and receive.

BOGUS FEEDBACK

Your credibility is one of the fundamental principles of effective feedback. Credibility is a function of competence, trustworthiness and goodwill. Hence, providing information about someone's performance that is incorrect, for one reason or another, is not good feedback.

Why would anyone give feedback that isn't true? There are more reasons for it than you may think. We will give you three: lack of skill, politics and skewed beliefs.

UNSKILLED

First, it can be a matter of skill. FairTalk needs you to observe performance, seek information from additional sources, align various inputs and distil all that into a few pithy statements. It requires some expertise. 'Winging it' may fall flat. Knowing the basics about feedback and using the proven techniques and models will certainly help. And there is no better teacher than practice and experience (and feedback!).

POLITICS

Another reason feedback may be bogus is political behaviour or attempts at manipulation. In 1987, an article was published called "Behind the Mask: The Politics of Employee Appraisal". Its findings hold true to this day – that is, managers manipulate performance information for political purposes.[147] They do it to avoid conflict, to safeguard resources, to appear in a more positive light or to avoid bureaucracy. It could also be related to efforts to assert and retain personal power.[148] Which ones have you observed recently?

Managers also fall prey to the status quo bias. This mental shortcut guards us from any action that may 'rock the boat' and change the established order of things. Whether it is done consciously or unconsciously, the result is bogus feedback.

SKEWED BELIEFS

Finally, bogus feedback can be the result of skewed beliefs about leadership, discussed in the introduction to Part One.

One such belief is that your employees are better off not knowing how they are doing.

Consider this example of a skewed belief. An employee is unlikely to be promoted. They don't have the leadership skills to take on a more senior position. But, if their manager tells them this, they will be demotivated. So the manager doesn't. The employee continues to work hard but doesn't work on their leadership skills and, funnily enough, does not advance! Self-fulfilling?

Some organizations use upward feedback in performance evaluations of their managers. This may mean that the opinions of the subordinates have a bearing on the performance evaluation of the boss. So, some managers may believe that by giving their employees the feedback they like (and not that they need) they will also get better reviews from their employees later. This is another example of a skewed belief. Basically, this leader is thinking, "Lying to my people to make them happy is justified by better evaluations from them later." Indeed, studies show that when employees are in a positive mood, they evaluate their leaders more favourably.[149] This is a sure recipe for mediocrity at best. Remember that fair, focused and credible feedback *also* make people more satisfied. Plus, more productive.

There is also the skewed belief that if a manager provides feedback that an employee is a poor performer, they will leave. Yup. But, as the old joke goes, if the manager doesn't give the feedback, the employee will stay!

BRUTAL FEEDBACK

To put this mildly, this is feedback that's crushingly upsetting.

Anecdotally, Winston Churchill was once confronted by a woman who declared that he was "disgustingly drunk".

Churchill responded: "My dear, you are ugly, and what's more, you are disgustingly ugly. But tomorrow I shall be sober, and you will still be ugly."[150] While it may have been honest, this was neither constructive nor useful feedback. It was crushing.

There is conclusive evidence that brutal feedback impairs trust, causes feelings of anger and increases blaming behaviours.[151] In most cases, such feedback is well intended but very badly executed. No matter the intent, brutal feedback is not fair. So, what makes us 'do a Churchill' from time to time?

Some of these tendencies are wired into our personality – some people naturally have a shorter fuse. Many Churchillian outbursts, however, are caused by fatigue, stress, jet lag, alcohol or drugs. With the exception of the last two, these pretty much describe the 'new normal' of today's organizational reality. Small wonder people say things they don't mean or don't want to say, and they come out as brutal feedback.

Have you ever said something that you have regretted afterwards? It could be as short as "Your work is rubbish" or "Even George from marketing would have done it better!" or "I guess you'll never learn to do it right..." Some are just naturally insensitive. But our bet is that, if you've ever said anything like this, either something got you really emotional so that you lost your cool, or you were not paying attention, were too complacent or didn't really care. Such feedback can be truly destructive – not only to the receiver but also to our own careers and relationships.

One night, the then CEO of Uber, Travis Kalanick, used his ride-sharing service with a driver by the name of Fawzi Kamel.[152] At the end of the ride, Kamel shared some unpleasant (but arguably true) information with Kalanick about his company: "But people are not trusting you anymore ... I lost $97,000 because of you. I'm bankrupt because of you." At the end of the conversation, Kalanick lost his temper and erupted destructively, "Some people don't like to take responsibility

for their own shit. They blame everything in their life on some-
body else. Good luck!" The conversation was video-recorded.
The driver turned it over to Bloomberg. That was the beginning
of the fall of Travis Kalanick.[153]

So, the best advice is to know your triggers and avoid them.
For instance, if you know that frequent interruptions get on
your nerves, plan to hold your feedback conversation in a
meeting room where others won't be looking for you, and leave
your phone behind. If you are very punctual and you don't like
to be late for your meetings, leave a buffer of time after the
performance discussion with your employee, or schedule it at
the end of the day, so that you are not pressed to finish it on
time. That way, if it goes on for slightly longer than planned,
it won't make you nervous.

If you catch yourself in 'brutal' mode, stop. Breathe. Correct yourself and redress the situation. And, if you have said
something unproductive already, remember, it is never too
late to apologize.

Mark Goulston, a business psychiatrist, outlines three steps
in apologizing meaningfully:[154]

1. Admit that you were wrong and that you are sorry.
2. Show the person you understand the effect your words
   or actions had on them.
3. Tell them what you are going to do differently in the
   future so that it does not happen again.

It is never too late to be fair.

KEY POINTS

Now you know that not all feedback is productive, you need to beware the types of feedback that produce no meaningful performance improvement. There are three types of bad feedback: baffling, bogus and brutal. *Baffling* feedback is useless (the person physically cannot do what you are asking), convoluted (you've been talking for an hour and the person has no idea what you are saying) or overwhelming (it's too much for the person to process right now!). *Bogus* feedback is information about performance that is not true. You may give bogus feedback because you lack training. Or you may distort the truth by being manipulative or playing politics. Finally, *brutal* feedback hurts unnecessarily and harms the relationship. Know your likely triggers to prevent yourself saying potentially destructive things and minimize their impact.

EXPERT'S OPINION

GIVING FEEDBACK TO DARK TRIAD LEADERS

Konstantin Korotov, professor, ESMT Berlin
Konstantin is professor, associate dean of executive education and
director of the Center for Leadership Development at ESMT Berlin. He
teaches executives about coping with the dark side of leadership, the
so-called Dark Triad – narcissism, Machiavellianism and psychopathy –
and how to work with those leaders.

**Sometimes we have to give feedback to those with very poor behaviours.
Before looking at how to do that, why keep such people in the organization
in the first place?**

Organizational life is extremely political and subjective. The Dark
Triad thrives in such murkiness. People with these characteristics
get results. Despite leadership development efforts, 'narcissistic
CEOs', 'snakes in suits' and 'psychopaths in the boardroom' are,
alas, still a norm today. To complicate matters, senior leaders
may consider some of the dark leadership traits as signposts of
potential; those who take charge (narcissists), influence effectively
(Machiavellians) and keep their cool amid havoc (psychopaths)
appear to embody attractive leadership behaviours. I teach how
to prevent overuse of these behaviours and save the executive
from derailment. Feedback plays a tremendous role.

**So, let's start with Machiavellianism. Who are those people
and how do you give feedback to them?**

The Machiavellians are characterized by an extreme degree of
pragmatism. They tend to be emotionally distant. For them the
end justifies the means. They are charming and hard to resist.
Organizations need politics because – hard truth – that is how

things get done. But problems emerge when political skills and power are used to advance personal interests to the detriment of the interests of the firm.

Since Machiavellians are, first and foremost, pragmatic, use numbers and figures when giving them feedback. Speak their language and link the feedback to their objectives. The underlying message would be, "You won't like it. But if you don't do it, you won't reach your goals." And one more thing – don't appeal to, or use, emotions. This is a wrong tactic with Machiavellians.

And what about feedback for psychopaths?

First, we are talking about the sub-clinical manifestation of psychopathy, as used in leadership research. With such leaders, say whatever you think. Most likely, they won't react emotionally. Their leadership style is characterized by a lack of care for others, lack of remorse when taking tough decisions and lack of guilt. Their approach is summarized in just two words – fearless dominance.

Psychopaths may listen to you and follow your advice. Some of your common-sense advice may be surprising to them, as they struggle to understand the emotional side of human relationships. Explain the costs of their decisions to them as seen by others.

Finally, let's talk about narcissism. The number of narcissists is on the rise.[155] How do we give feedback to them?

Narcissists have an inflated view of their own importance, with a sense of entitlement and willingness to exploit others. Such high self-esteem may turn into an autocratic, impulsive, controlling style, with poor listening and low empathy – also known as hubris.

Science says that it's useless to give them feedback. Narcissism is linked to a deep fear of being inadequate. Feedback that is threatening leads to an aggressive defensive reaction. Feedback presented as developmental may be more digestible for a narcissist. Sometimes a better strategy may be limiting their access to the limelight rather than trying to change them.

CHAPTER 9

Trap 2: Emotions.
Keep Calm and Give Feedback

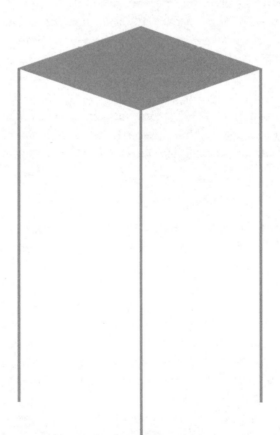

"While it's not surprising that people avoid offering and receiving feedback, its performance-boosting power can't be left to the insecurities and emotions of individual leaders."[156]

Marc Effron, talent consultant

Emotion is perhaps the biggest obstacle to quality performance-enhancing feedback.

An employee may get emotional, defensive or even angry when they hear tough messages about how they performed. Especially if those messages contradict their own view of themselves. It takes a lot of emotional maturity to consider feedback your friend.

Ironically enough, the emotion that often prevents feedback is not the emotion of the receiver. It is the emotion of the giver.

> *You have to be real about what feedback is. It's not a comfortable process. It is never going to be palatable to tell people what they are not good at. Don't have unrealistic expectations that it's going to be something they will be looking forward to. It won't be an easy conversation. But it will be very helpful.*[157]

Giving feedback is a leadership task. Emotion, if it prevents us from giving feedback, reduces our ability to be effective leaders. So what do you do?

The good news is that managing emotions is a learnable skill. Based on our competency model (see Chapter 2), we call this 'resilient'. It is the ability to keep calm and composed, especially in high-intensity and stressful situations. As we said, if you can name it, you can work it!

To be more resilient in feedback, consider:

- **Preparation**. Know, cold, what you are going to say – keep it to the FairTalk Statement if that is easier – then you leave yourself room to manage the emotional issues a little better. Following the advice in Chapters 6 and 7 will ensure great preparation.
- **Practice**. This takes us from being able to have one effective feedback conversation to building competence. You will become a leader who has the skills and behaviours required to give great feedback.

That leaves dealing with your emotions.

WHAT MAKES IT EMOTIONALLY HARD?

We all handle emotions differently. Being aware of this already makes giving feedback easier.

In considering the impact of emotions, one challenge is that we all start from different baselines. You may naturally be wired to handle difficult conversations better than others. Your personality may make it easier for you to control your emotions (psychologists would call you 'better adjusted'), so giving or receiving feedback is a piece of cake, right? But this isn't true for those of us who are not so well adjusted, who are prone to self-doubt and more easily stressed. Or for those who are highly sensitive, empathetic, diplomatic or caring.

There are two characteristics of feedback that make it difficult for almost anyone to give and hear. One relates to the relationship and the other to the message itself.

Consciously or subconsciously, feedback is perceived as a threat to a *relationship* – something that we, as social beings, try to avoid. This is a struggle between two opposing basic human needs: getting ahead and getting along.[158] Driving performance is fuelled by the 'getting ahead' motivation (drive, getting better, reaching goals, personal growth), while the 'getting along' motives call for avoiding confrontation to maintain the relationship. Learning to effectively navigate this tension is key to giving high-quality feedback:

> *The risk of harming one's relationships looms larger than the risks to the recipients' performance and careers. But leaders forget that they have a mandate to develop others.*[159]

The second shared difficulty in delivering feedback has to do with the contents of the *message*. Feedback is distinct from any other type of information in one important aspect: it is evaluative. And, since evaluation implies passing judgement, it puts our ego and self-image at stake. This makes things more emotional, and people do not like dealing with emotions.

A study conducted with supervisors at a counselling practice discovered that giving feedback to their supervisees on clinical topics (e.g. work process or a specific client) was much easier than giving feedback on personal topics (e.g. relationships or behaviours).[160] The same study demonstrated that the difficulty of giving feedback increased in line with its subjectivity. (Chapter 6 is full of tips on aligning your feedback to improve accuracy and remove subjectivity.)

These considerations impact your effectiveness at giving feedback. And then personality comes into play.

INTERPERSONAL SENSITIVITY

As we have said, some personality types have the positive attributes of diplomacy, tactfulness and sensitivity. These are all great qualities, but they are not necessarily the most helpful in giving feedback. Those who are highly sensitive to the feelings and reactions of others are naturally averse to conveying tough messages.

Asking people to do what is innately tough for them is not typically a winning strategy.

But, fortunately, having coached a lot of leaders, including those who find giving feedback challenging, we have found that you can use people's sensitivity as the reason to give feedback, rather than the reason not to.

This is called "reframing". To reframe is to change our perspective, even though the facts don't change. Instead, we shift how we interpret those facts.

If you are highly interpersonally sensitive, this practical reframing exercise will help you in your battle with making a decision about whether to say something or not:

> By not saying what I honestly see, I am at best misleading this person and at worst lying by omission.
>
> By misleading them in this way, I am not helping them deal with something that may be challenging and difficult for them right now.
>
> By not helping them deal with what challenges them, I am reducing their ability to be high performing.
>
> By reducing their ability to be high performing, I am potentially impacting their ability to have the fullest career possible.

> I want this person to genuinely like me. Would they like me if they knew that I misled them and as a result reduced their ability to perform and succeed?
>
> Is that the caring person that I am?

Does this make a difference? In our experience, it does.

IMD professor George Kohlrieser teaches about the importance of being a 'secure base' for your employees. Making a parallel with mountain climbing, secure base leadership is about supporting and protecting your people from the safety of the base camp so that they can climb higher and perform at their peak. According to Kohlrieser, giving regular feedback, no matter how hard it is, is one of the landmarks of such leadership: "Sometimes it is better to be slapped by the truth than kissed with a lie."[161]

Now, you can use this reframing exercise in coaching conversations with your sensitive team members who struggle to give tough feedback.

PERFORMANCE ANXIETY

Some personality types have the positive attributes of conscientiousness, concern for results and genuine worry that things may go wrong. These are all great qualities too, but not necessarily the most helpful when giving feedback.

Asking these personality types to do what is likely to disrupt short-term results, or what is risky, is innately tough for them and therefore, again, not typically a winning strategy.

Fortunately, we have also coached a lot of these leaders. We use their performance anxiety as a reason to give feedback, rather than the reason not to.

If you are this personality type, here's an exercise in reframing for you:

By not saying what I honestly see, I may be risking further mistakes and errors.

By risking further mistakes and errors, I am jeopardizing future performance.

By jeopardizing future performance, I compromise the performance of the team, and I am responsible and accountable for that.

By compromising my accountability to drive high performance, I undermine my position as a leader.

Is this the high-performance leader that I am?

If you are sensitive or have anxiety that feedback will impact short-term performance, maybe giving feedback will never be your forte. But this way of reframing feedback has helped many leaders embrace giving feedback – if not happily, at least stoically.

Here is a tip. If one of your direct reports isn't good at feedback, and if that has to be the subject of *your* feedback to them, use a FairTalk Statement. For example, you could say:

Honest feedback is important. Without it, you risk mistakes, jeopardize future performance and compromise the results of the team, for which you are accountable. You are not giving your team members clear feedback. My expectation is that you set a specific goal to learn to improve the frequency and quality of the feedback you give to your team.

This is FairTalk.

UNDERSTANDING THE EMOTIONS OF OTHERS

Another way of reducing your emotions is to proactively plan for the emotions of others. This is part of your preparation.

Getting feedback can be emotionally taxing for the receiver, too. Some receivers are 'easier' than others. It is much easier to give feedback to someone who wants to hear it and will be grateful for the fair message no matter how tough it is. Scientists have singled out five characteristics that tell us whether someone will have a positive attitude towards feedback.[162] We have turned them into a short exercise for you.

Think of an employee to whom you need to deliver a piece of feedback. Now answer these five questions to determine whether the message is likely to land well:

	YES	NO
1. Does this person believe in the value of feedback?		
2. Is this person curious to learn how others view their performance, even if it is constructive criticism?		
3. Does this person process feedback intentionally, taking a balanced view of their own performance?		

4. Is this person self-aware? (In other words, does this person know both their own strengths and weaknesses and how others perceive them?)		
5. Would this person typically take accountability to act on feedback?		

The more 'yeses' there are, the easier it will be to deliver feedback to this person. Curious people are less defensive and less prone to aggression in the face of provocation.[163] Greater self-awareness means that there will be fewer surprises. Valuing feedback and taking accountability for improvement naturally lead to greater performance.[164] You probably won't even break a sweat giving feedback to those who score five out of five.

Potentially, however, it is when there are several 'no' answers that this practical tool becomes of most value. It signals a potential barrier and arms you with early information that can help you to handle the situation effectively as part of your preparation. When you get a 'no', reflect on what may make the task emotionally easier for you.

Thinking about the receptivity of the receiver allows you to modify your messages, while keeping consistent with the FairTalk Statement.

USING EMOTIONS TO GET
EVEN BETTER RESULTS

We fear feedback because we fear the effect it may have on others. We may therefore be tempted to think that emotions are all bad. However, when it comes to feedback, emotions in others can also be our friend. There are two key reasons for this.

The first reason is that *emotion is highly correlated with memory*. Adding balanced, emotional language to your Fair-Talk Statement will make the feedback you give even more memorable. Studies confirm that feedback delivered with a balance of positive and negative language has the greatest impact on employees' decisions to incorporate suggestions and make revisions.[165] So review your feedback. When you see a meaningful performance improvement opportunity, don't be concerned about including negative language. When you see what you expect, don't hold back on the positives.

Even beyond the language, adding a strong emotion will make the message more memorable – full stop. Of course, as a general rule, your feedback should be respectful and not personal. But a dose of 'righteous indignation' could also be fair, couldn't it? In a conversation we had with Lucien Alziari, CHRO of Prudential, he reflected:

As human beings, we are not at our best all the time. As a leader, you won't always get it right. You always have a vested interest either in the outcome or in the individual. You want to choose a moment when you are calm and controlled. But when you come back to that underlying principle that you have their best interests are at heart, it still works. A little bit of emotion or strength of feeling can create more trust. As long as it's not an exercise in humiliation. Sometimes a bit of amplification does not hurt, usually because of the importance of the issue, or the individual, or both.[166]

The second reason the emotions of others can be our friend is that *our message is understood through more than just our words*. While we should be clear with our feedback and expectations, we don't have to lack empathy. So long as it is in keeping with the situation, empathy can be extremely helpful, both in managing emotions and in the overall outcome. Daniel Goleman, the father of emotional intelligence, affirms that empathy is a critical element in delivering feedback.

He quotes an interesting study on the topic, where two groups were compared:

One [group] received negative performance feedback accompanied by positive emotional signals – namely, nods and smiles; the other was given positive feedback that was delivered critically, with frowns and narrowed eyes ... The people who had received positive feedback accompanied by negative emotional signals reported feeling worse about their performance than did the participants who had received good-natured negative feedback. In effect, the delivery was more important than the message itself.[167]

In other words, our nonverbal cues, where congruent with our message, help receivers better understand our feedback.

One final preparation worth considering is preparing for how the unexpected emotions of others can cause unexpected emotions in... you.

Getting feedback can be an affective experience, especially if the feedback is unpalatable. People will react. If people react in ways that differ from what we expect, we can judge the receiver harshly, not necessarily because of the reaction but because it was unexpected.

For example, we may have an expectation that men and women deal with feedback differently. The expectation that a man will get angry and a woman might cry is stereotypical. We might expect these reactions. But what happens when the responses don't align with our expectations?

In an article called "Boys, Don't Cry: Gender and Reactions to Negative Performance Feedback", the authors found that biases are ripe and rife in organizations:

When men cry ... they are labeled as atypical, which has consequences for how others evaluate them at work, leading to lower performance evaluations and assessments of leadership capability, and a more negative tone in letters of recommendation.[168]

In other words, considering *likely* emotions helps us prepare. But failing to consider *unlikely* emotions may cause us to be caught off guard, which may negatively impact how we assess the receiver and deliver the feedback.

Understanding our emotions and the emotions of others makes us more effective; bar none. This is a book about feedback in organizations so our emphasis is the emotional side of delivering difficult performance information. But the same principles hold true for any difficult conversation at work. And even outside. Getting better at giving feedback will not only make you a better boss but also a better spouse, sibling, child, parent and friend.

KEY POINTS

Being emotionally resilient is a trainable skill and you can get better at it. Preparation and practice reduce the cognitive and emotional strain of feedback, leaving you to deal with the emotional challenge. Some people are naturally better at dealing with emotions than others. In any case, feedback is emotional because it may impact the relationship and it often requires us to deliver evaluative judgements, which is uncomfortable. Reframing helps us to deal with two of the most common emotional barriers to giving feedback: interpersonal sensitivity and performance anxiety. Leveraging emotions can even be advantageous, as they make feedback memorable. While the emotional challenge is unlikely to go away, reframing feedback and preparing for the emotional responses of others have helped many leaders.

EXPERT'S OPINION

STAYING COOL WHEN DELIVERING HOT MESSAGES

Linda Rodman, president, Rodman Resources LLC
Linda is an executive coach and leadership consultant with over 20,000 hours of related coaching. She is passionately engaged in enabling leaders to achieve their highest potential personally, and through others. In many cases this includes teaching them how to deliver high impact feedback and coaching – subjects about which she has spoken and written extensively.

Drawing lessons from thousands of pieces of constructive feedback provided over decades of coaching, I would add four capabilities that are necessary for staying calm when delivering feedback.

1. Believing in the value of constructive feedback

Often I ask people if they like giving negative feedback. Generally, they do not, and provide answers such as: "I don't want to hurt their feelings" or "I can't demotivate them now!" This is similar to thinking that by staying away from the doctor's office you can avoid being ill.

Developing an unshakeable belief in the beneficial power of feedback is a sure-fire way of calming your anxieties. It makes it easier to accurately weigh the risks and rewards of speaking up.

2. Simultaneously co-creating effective paths forward

Another reason for feeling anxious is the worry that people won't change, even when you go out on a limb. To avoid this, feedback should be accompanied by simultaneous coaching.

I recommend a 10% *retrospective* feedback and 90% *prospective* collaborative problem-solving time ratio to ensure that dialogues are both comfortable and enabling. These conversations work best if you identify the issues, ask whether the person agrees, resolve misalignments, solicit improvement ideas, discuss and modify these, and offer suggestions.

3. Disarming the recipient's emotional reactions

When people get upset, it's easy to lose composure. There are some 'tough love' ways of preventing this, which have to include the 'love' component to be successful.

- **Show you care**. Continually demonstrate that you want to set them up for success. If your interactions are infrequent, start by describing that the feedback is intended to help them succeed, without any ulterior motive.
- **Play on their team**. When people hear negative feedback, they feel lessened and vulnerable. It is essential to help them restore their equilibrium by expressing genuine empathy. Instead of saying niggling things start on *their* side – for example, "You have every reason to be upset" or "The substance of your position is right." Once you have established-team alignment, candidly describe the specific problematic behaviours and how they will impact achievement of the person's goals.
- **Be respectful**. If you're upset, postpone conveying your feedback until you can express your thoughts in a constructive way. Would the recipient think you were on their side? If not, know there is no shame in delaying for even a few days.

4. The power of visioning

The research findings are compelling: visioning works! Before giving feedback, envision yourself delivering challenging messages in a calm and collected manner. Envision your words, tone, posture, facial expression, gestures, breathing, etc. while delivering the feedback and handling possible bad reactions. If you can't see that picture clearly in your mind, imagine yourself at the beach relaxing under a palm tree with a fresh wind blowing and making you feel *cool* and comfortable despite the sweltering climate and *hot* sun.

CHAPTER 10

Trap 3: Context.
Giving Feedback Across Boundaries

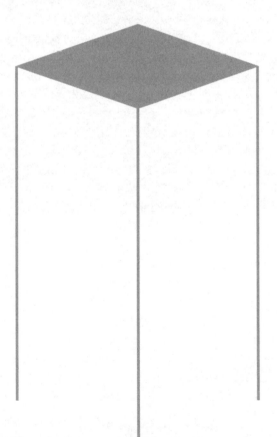

"It's very important to know the neighbour next door and the people down the street and the people in another race."[169]

Maya Angelou

The world is flat.[170] Globalization, technology, automated workflows, crowdsourcing – all this rapid change is making giving feedback easier. And harder, too...

Giving feedback can be simple. You diagnose the situation. You craft a powerful FairTalk Statement. And you prepare to deliver it, using emotions to your advantage. Before beginning, do one more thing: check the boundaries.

There are interpersonal boundaries, such as gender, age and culture. When you are preparing to give feedback to an individual, you will want to consider these factors.

There are also boundaries caused by the way work is structured. You will want to consider how feedback is delivered and received when the context is within a team or across a hierarchy.

INTERPERSONAL BOUNDARIES

GENDER DIFFERENCES

Do men and women treat feedback differently? In short, yes.

A full answer would require a few more chapters and is not straightforward. But we want to provide a few researched examples that confirm how feedback behaviours and reactions differ in men and women. Then we'll try to make each piece of information practical.

Studies suggest that men may be more *protective of their reputation* than women. They may fail to ask for feedback, even if they badly need it. Practically speaking, you will want to give feedback to the men on your team proactively. Don't wait to be asked.

Women are more driven by the expertise of the feedback giver (their credibility, as discussed in Chapter 4) than by the fear of appearing incompetent – unless (and here is a complexity) that expert is another female.[171] What does all this mean in practical terms? If you are a male supervisor, it is likely that your female subordinates will proactively seek and listen to your feedback. If you are a female leader, actively work on ensuring there are open channels of communication with your female employees.

Research also confirms that women are more attuned to information about *their* performance, while men tend to care more how others are doing. When feedback about below-average performance is given to a woman, she sees it as an indication of her overall ability.[172] There are practical implications for the leader. When giving feedback to women, watch for the tendency that they may generalize your feedback. The generalization may make your feedback overwhelming and blur the focus on what needs to be improved. So keep it very specific.

There are also differences in how the genders respond to feedback that is relative to others. Select research showed that women generally were less likely than men to take on a challenge that had some risk.[173] When relative performance feedback was provided to the female participants with above-average results (e.g. "You are doing better than 70% of the group"), decisions to participate (take on the challenge) increased by nearly 20%. The practical application? If you are giving feedback to a higher-performing woman, tell her she is higher performing. She is simply more likely to take on the challenge of further improving. But, while that relative performance information is beneficial for higher-performing women, it may lead to self-doubt and lower self-esteem in lower-performing women. The practical implication? Compare her performance to her own past, better performances. Or to the results you expected. Just don't make comparisons to others.

In the same study, men (including below-average performers) were found to have a greater propensity to take on the challenge right from the beginning. Giving these men feedback on their relative performance had no significant effect on whether they took up the challenge.[174] So just give the feedback.

Another distinction in giving feedback across genders is called the 'surprise effect'. Researchers have discovered that women are more likely to change their behaviour when they receive feedback they do not expect[175] – that is, when they hear and respond to a new insight. From a practical point of view, consider what could add this element of surprise: sharing a new source for the feedback, reframing the message, providing fresh examples or pointing out consequences that may not have been discussed before. These tactics add a new element to the feedback and, the research suggests, this increases the likelihood of positive change. Don't confuse 'surprised' with "What the #$%@?" Chapter 8 specifically talks about the negative impact of overwhelming feedback. And this certainly isn't an excuse to 'save up' your feedback and to deliver it at year end while yelling "Surprise!"

Interestingly, this 'surprise effect' was not found in men. So again – just tell them!

This is, by no means, an extensive overview of gender differences in seeking and receiving feedback. Our goal is to bring to light the fact that there are meaningful differences (see TABLE 5 next page).

Yet, when in doubt, stick to the FairTalk Statement. Trust that outlining the powerful *why*, being clear about current performance and crafting clear expectations of what your employees should do in the future will prevail over individual differences.

TABLE 5: Six academic research findings at a glance: gender and feedback

WOMEN	MEN
1. More likely to ask for feedback	1. Less likely to ask for feedback
2. Respond positively to an expert giving the feedback, especially male	2. Less driven by the expertise of the feedback giver
3. Like absolute feedback about their performance	3. Like to understand how they compare to others
4. See feedback about low performance as a reflection of their overall ability	4. Driven to improve by feedback about low performance
5. Find relative performance information either helpful (high-performing women) or not helpful (low-performing women)	5. Like comparing their performance to others (true for both high- and low-performing men)
6. More likely to act on feedback they do not expect	6. Unaffected by feedback novelty in terms of its impact on desire to change

GIVING FEEDBACK ACROSS GENERATIONS

When people ask us how to give feedback to millennials, our standard answer is, "Privately, with tact and following the FairTalk Statement. Just like you would to anyone else, right?"

Beware the generational difference myth. A lot of hype surrounds the challenges of dealing with these so-called self-centred, highly sensitive and disloyal millennials! Much of the hype is myth, in many cases blown out of proportion by the leadership development and consulting industries. In one of the most thorough studies of its kind (reported in a meta-analytical study[176] and a recent focal research paper[177]), Dr David Costanza from George Washington University and his colleagues definitively debunked the common mis-conception that there are notable and significant differences in job satisfaction, organizational loyalty or turnover intent attributable solely to being born a few decades earlier or later.

The practical implication is clear. If you have been putting off tough feedback because of a fear of its impact on a member of Generation Y or a millennial, don't.

Instead, follow our approach. If experience, not age, is a modifier, temper your feedback appropriately (Chapter 4). Feedback will sound, look and feel different when it is deliv-ered to a seasoned professional. And in both cases the general principle holds: "Tell me why it matters," "Tell me how I'm doing" and "Tell me what to do" (Chapter 7).

CULTURAL ASPECTS OF FEEDBACK

You don't have to have employees from another country to still need to know about culture. You could have international vendors. Or customers. Or clients. Maybe you are from the north and your employee is from the south. Every one of us is part of the global marketplace, one way or another, and cultural nuances are increasingly important in how we work today.

Just in our combined experience, of living and working in nine countries and four continents, we were able to come up with more than a dozen general manager appointments that failed due to a lack of intercultural awareness. In just ten minutes. Most often, the reason is an inability to lead people in a different culture.

Erin Meyer, a professor of organizational behaviour at INSEAD, is an expert on intercultural management. Her best-selling book *The Culture Map* is a useful companion for anyone doing business with people from different cultural origins from their own.[178] The book and the accompanying diagnostic tool are the culmination of years of research, interviews and observations on how human interactions play out in diverse cultural settings.

One of the scales in *The Culture Map* is fully dedicated to giving negative feedback. That scale is called Evaluating, and it deals with a preference for frank versus diplomatic negative feedback:

Managers in different parts of the world are conditioned to give feedback in dramatically different ways. In general, the Thai manager learns never to criticize a colleague openly or in front of others, while the Dutch manager learns to be as honest as possible and give the message straight. The French are generally taught to criticize passionately and provide positive feedback sparingly, while Americans commonly learn to give three positives with every negative and call people out for doing things right (which can be downright confounding to many raised in other cultures).[179]

As we do, *The Culture Map* advises against jumping into generalizations and stereotypes, but rather reinforces the need to be open-minded.

The good news, coming from research, is that co-workers of different nationalities are more likely to seek feedback from each other.[180] A combination of natural curiosity and the psychological need to reduce uncertainty makes us more attuned to feedback from those who are different from us.

The most famous and arguably most widely used classification of cultures stems from Geert Hofstede's research. A former IBM employee, he became interested in workplace issues resulting from the simple fact that people came from different countries. He analysed cultures around the world and identified six dimensions of culture, such as Power Distance, Individualism vs Collectivism, Masculinity vs Femininity and others.[181]

While feedback practices across cultures are outside of the scope of this book, we want you to be aware of key differences. TABLE 6 illustrates how feedback approaches may vary across intercultural contexts and offers some practical tips for further improving your feedback.

TABLE 6: Cultural differences in giving feedback

FEEDBACK PRINCIPLE[182]	HOFSTEDE'S CULTURAL DIMENSION	EXAMPLE COUNTRIES	TIPS FOR FAIRTALK FEEDBACK
FAIRNESS	**High feminine culture** (cooperative, caring, striving for work–life balance)	Netherlands, Norway, Sweden	Signal that you give feedback because you want the person to be successful and have the collective best interest at heart.
	High indulgence (quick gratification, enjoying life, optimism)	Australia, Brasil, Nigeria, UK, USA	Deliver even negative feedback with a positive attitude; allow the employee to voice their reaction.
FOCUS	**High uncertainty avoidance** (preference for strict codes, rules and procedures; there is one 'truth')	Germany, France, Japan, Mexico, South Korea	Be extremely clear, specific, and follow the FairTalk Statement.
	Long-term orientation (valuing pragmatism and perseverance, orientation towards future rewards)	Germany, Italy, Japan, Russia, Sweden	Explain why it matters and link the feedback to better performance outcomes. Establish clear expectations.
CREDIBILITY	**High collectivism** (relationships are integrated; groups are tightly knit)	China, Mexico, Russia, Turkey, Vietnam	Make sure that you establish strong interpersonal connections and that you are perceived as part of the same, bigger team.
	Low power distance (authority is questioned and hierarchies are flattened)	Austria, Denmark, Israel	Allow for opportunities for people to express their own views and come up with ways of improvement.

The fairness principle of FairTalk (Chapter 4) says that feedback is intended to make people successful. The FairTalk Statement does that. And, if you can emphasize the part of the statement that is especially meaningful to the culture of your team member, you have an even greater chance of effecting positive change.

Other things you can do as a leader to better allow for global differences include constantly adjusting and re-adjusting your understanding of other cultures. Value the role of training on cultural differences and set expectations for your team to be cross-culturally sensitive.

Combining cultural perspectives complicates things. Those of us who like structure and specificity are going haywire about now. Yet this is the reality of doing business today for many of us. Stay focused and stay flexible.

ORGANIZATIONAL BOUNDARIES

We have been talking about giving feedback across interpersonal boundaries. There is another type of boundary. It is created by how we organize work: in teams and organizations.

FEEDBACK AMONG THE TEAM

Should you share information about an individual's performance with the team? You will hear that feedback needs to be given only in private. This is another case of "Yes, but..." There is academic and empirical evidence that feedback on individuals, shared with the team, can be extremely effective for an individual's performance.

A paper published in 2017 in the journal *Management Science* confirmed the benefits of sharing individuals' relative performance within a group of employees. Being able to see who the top performers are allowed the lower-performing colleagues to identify the best practices of their more productive peers and copy them. Such an approach also created social pressure to increase the level of performance. It resulted in a 10.9% improvement in productivity just because of this simple practice.[183]

This is not new. The Haier Group Corporation, a Chinese multinational home appliances company, has been providing its employees with openly shared performance feedback information for over 30 years.[184] In 2015, Haier's CEO Zhang Ruimin was awarded a Global CEO Award for Innovative Talent Management Practices.[185] This is an example of a company that is unafraid of staying the course and sticking to its practices – even if that means publicly displaying individual KPIs (key performance indicators).

While we don't necessarily advocate sharing à la Haier, don't discount the value of letting people know where they stand relative to others. It won't always have negative consequences. Consider *practical* adaptations of the principle of transparency.

Share what good looks like

Calling out the highest performers publicly, and having them share some of their practices, can be rewarding for the individual. The result can be shared learning, adding to team productivity.

Optimize face-to-face time

In-person meetings are especially great for teams that work remotely. Research confirms that the less facetime employees have with their managers, the more impact seeking and receiving feedback will have on their performance.[186] Unfortunately, the agendas of meetings are almost always filled with operational business topics. Find time for team building. Stronger interpersonal relationships and trust among team members will greatly facilitate giving feedback later, when people are far away from each other again.

Put in place processes to make team feedback easy

Make time in team meetings for peer feedback sharing. At first, it may be awkward. Make it non-threatening and fun. Consider adapting the FairTalk Statement ("Tell me why it matters," "Tell me how I'm doing" and "Tell me what to do") to increase the quality of feedback while using the time effectively. You don't have to call it feedback. Call it a 'post-mortem'. Or an 'after-action review'. Team debriefings on what went wrong and what went right have been used in medical and military settings for years, and successfully. Meta-analytical evidence suggests that, in business settings, individual and team reviews of results lead to 20-25% increases in performance.[187]

In the 1970s, the US Army was desperate for a way to make learning a key part of its culture. Its leaders chose to implement something called 'performance critiques'. Designated observers would watch training exercises and deliver detailed assessments after the fact. It was an epic failure. The participants felt demeaned and dispirited and little learning emerged. In search of a better solution, the army decided to experiment with something called 'after-action reviews'. After any kind of activity, the participants gather and discuss these simple questions:

1. What was our objective?
2. What happened?
3. What did we learn?
4. What will we do differently next time?
5. When is an opportunity coming to try this different approach?[188]

Leverage technology

There are a number of social collaboration platforms, as well as specific applications, that allow for feedback to be shared with a person, even in real time. Crowdsourced feedback can help a manager to address the results and behaviours that are not directly visible due to the remote nature of work.

You may be labelled a maverick – or, as Francesca Gino calls it in her recent book with the same name,[189] a 'rebel talent'. The wider culture may not be conducive to calling out those who do well and those who hold the team back. While you may not be in a position to change your organizational policies and practices, you can start by providing group feedback to your own team – adjusting, of course, for what is practical and reasonable.

FEEDBACK UP, SIDEWAYS AND AROUND

In earlier chapters, we commented that there is a deficit of feedback in organizations. It is particularly scarce at higher levels. The higher you go, the less feedback you get. Sadly, it is when you need it most.

Early in their career, people need to know how they are doing, so they can build managerial and technical competencies. Minor mistakes are opportunities to learn. For senior leaders, who may not get feedback on their decisions and behaviours, failure to get feedback may mean career derailment.

One of us recalled the following email from a participant in a leadership training course at a prestigious business school. This person was a mid-level manager at a large company:

In the program, we discussed how to motivate subordinates. However, I am thinking now how to thank my boss. Could you tell me if there are any techniques to express gratitude to a superior? I am always afraid that this will be misunderstood and taken for flattery. Are there any anonymous ways to let my boss know that one of his subordinates is genuinely grateful to him? Or is it a wrong approach and bosses should not be praised? Please let me know if this is an acceptable practice and how I can do it.

It may seem odd that an employee would feel concerned about giving positive feedback. The disappointing but prevailing organizational reality is that employees are sometimes better off keeping their opinions to themselves, no matter how negative, positive, creative or otherwise.[190]

But we believe in FairTalk. So, what advice did we give to this manager?

Use the FairTalk Statement, merely adjusting it to suit the purpose. For example:

1. Say why it matters (to you).
2. Say what and how your boss is doing (and the impact it has had on you and your ability to deliver the results).
3. Say what your boss could do differently in the future (and why it will make you more productive).

Several weeks later another email from the participant arrived:

You cannot imagine how successful it was! I was talking to my boss. Obviously, when you deal with superiors much more senior than you, you are afraid to come across as sucking up. Unexpectedly, he visited our office and we had a few minutes together. First, we discussed the pending business issues and then I told him everything just as planned :) Our boss is a very 'closed person'. He is often described as a poker face. He seldom smiles, but during our conversation I noticed a glimpse.

The simple FairTalk messaging structure opened up a whole channel of communication, further built the relationship and contributed to the organizational habit of giving feedback.

So adopt the right mindset: bosses need to hear feedback, too!

The same goes for feedback among peers. The FairTalk model takes the heat out of those difficult conversations. A lot of time spent together in meetings and socializing makes it easier for peers to discuss what went right and what went wrong in their recent interactions. Research confirms that peer feedback is important.

Earlier we said that self-perception of performance is often the least accurate. A meta-analysis looking at feedback data from various sources found that we rarely see ourselves as our peers see us. But the way our peers see us correlates much more strongly with the views of our boss.[191] In other words, your peers can be a great source of information on your performance. The added benefit is that it may be much less stressful to hear it from a team member than from the boss.

Quite a distinct issue is giving feedback to a person who is not your boss, your subordinate, your peer or your team member, but anyone else who contributes to the success of the same organization. The most common answer we hear is, "It's not up to me."

Yes, it is up to you, if you care about the organization and your working environment.

And you would want someone to give you feedback on your performance, and on how you could get better, if the alternative was that your performance was the subject of gossip or complaints by others.

So here are a few ways that you can go about this:

- Ask the person whether they would like to hear some feedback. We bet you that most people will say, "Yes, please."
- If for some reason you choose to provide feedback anonymously, use existing channels. If there is a feedback app or an established practice of giving each other performance information, use that.
- In extreme cases, you may need to give feedback to the person's boss with a few succinct details. Explain when and where the issue happened, and use the FairTalk Statement: concentrate on why it matters, how the person did and what could be done differently in the future. But, even when you need to involve someone else's boss, be upfront and transparent about it. You wouldn't want anyone going to your boss behind your back with critical feedback about you. Rather, try what Fred Kofman from Google calls "clean escalation".[192] Call a three-way meeting and have a FairTalk conversation together.

In summary, when we talk about feedback, it is not necessarily top-down communication. In supportive environments, performance information flows freely and eagerly in all directions.[193]

FROM GENERALIZATION
TO FAIRTALK

There is no absence of data on how different groups respond to feedback. We have shared some of the most important findings. There is a cognitive ease that comes from applying stereotypes. This is the case whether the stereotypes are false (baby boomers need security) or well researched (men are less likely to ask for feedback). However, generalizations are just that.

We share the research only in the context of the bigger FairTalk model. In formulating your feedback, you will *already* have taken into account experience, personality, business environment and more. Without these considerations, you will be using generalizations about what drives performance in different groups, and this won't result in FairTalk. Rather, properly prepared FairTalk that gives *additional* consideration to these factors will be all the more powerful and effective.

The FairTalk model encourages leaders to tailor their approach and messaging to each individual person and situation. This is far more effective than relying on hackneyed stereotypes.

KEY POINTS

Feedback takes place in a context. The context could involve differences between individuals, such as age, or the nature of relationships, such as being peers. A well-prepared FairTalk Statement is always a good foundation for feedback. However, that feedback can be modified to better manage the existing social and organizational boundaries. The findings we share are based on research. Such knowledge can be helpful, enabling us to modify feedback for greater success. However, while useful, it does not necessarily tell us how any one person may respond to feedback. Your knowledge of your team members, as their leader, is critical.

EXPERT'S OPINION

ACCELERATING ORGANIZATIONS THROUGH FEEDBACK

Ellen Maag, partner, Heidrick & Struggles
Ellen is the Americas regional lead for Heidrick & Struggles'
Leadership and Development Center of Excellence. Heidrick &
Struggles is a leading company in executive search and leadership
development. Ellen works with senior executives around the world
on projects ranging from leadership assessment, development and
succession to global enterprise transformation.

How do today's complex organizational structures affect feedback?

In higher-performing organizations, the formality of the structure or hierarchy doesn't seem to make much of a difference to the effectiveness of feedback. One of my clients is a traditional oil and gas company established more than 100 years ago. Feedback flows naturally from top to bottom, bottom to top and side to side. Senior leaders solicit feedback from subordinates. Candour and courage are two of the company's values. Conversely, I've worked with a younger tech firm that has a pretty flat structure and a hip, open working environment but an almost non-existent ability to have candid conversations about performance and behaviour.

What are these types of organization doing to cause feedback to "flow naturally"?

My colleagues and I have researched what the highest-performing global companies do better than their competitors. One of the factors that emerged is the ability to 'robustly challenge' one another.

More and more, we see these organizations recognizing that building stronger 'feedback muscle' is one of the key levers they can pull to accelerate performance. NASA, at least by some, is credited as one of the first users of the term 'feedback'. Whether this is true or not, I've always liked the metaphor of providing a rocket with 'on-course' and 'off-course' feedback. A rocket's journey is subject to atmospheric conditions: the context. Agile organizations understand, as NASA did, that waiting to 'correct' an object's (or person's) path until the very end of the journey will more likely end in a Mars landing than a lunar one.

We also found it is equally important to appreciate and affirm. In feedback, two good things for every negative thing can be the rule of thumb. When you wait until there is a crisis of performance, that balance gets much more difficult to strike.

How else does the context influence the feedback experience? Can technology help?

We need to be wary. Feedback done well is a very personal experience. As you rightly point out in this book, it needs to be timely. It is best done face to face. It needs to be delivered with some consideration for a receiver's readiness to hear it. Today there are many technological solutions that pretend to do that. My fear is that technology makes it all too easy to blast off an email without a thought of how it will come across or the impact it will have. If you provide feedback without having to look the person in the eye, it can be hard to achieve the desired balance of support and challenge that leads to real growth.

And, while I am believer in the great tools we now have to collect 360-degree feedback – I use them daily in my work – I can see there is some risk. We might be overly quick to take the data these surveys provide at face value without fully understanding the context of the individual or the tone or intent of the feedback.

CHAPTER 11

Anyone Can
Change

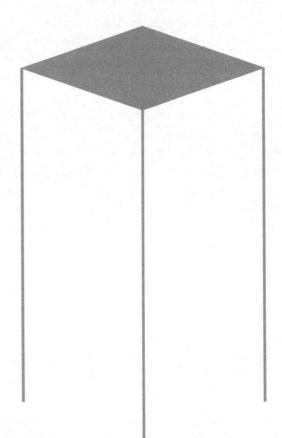

"The key to all of this – to how natural selection is able to produce its wondrous results – is the power of many, many small but cumulative changes."[194]

Helena Cronin, Darwinian philosopher

As discussed, change is hard. A critical question is: can people really change at all? The answer is unambiguous – everyone has the ability to change. Change is supported by our very biology and is enhanced when we have the right mindset.

WHAT DOES THE BIOLOGY SAY?

Knowledge, skills and attitudes are not part of our DNA. They are acquired with experience. There is solid science to prove that anyone can develop and grow.

A University of Minnesota study compared 238 identical male twins to 188 fraternal twins and found that genetic factors account for 30% of why someone is in a leadership role.[195] A follow-up study on female twins took this small DNA impact out of the equation. It was experience, personality and deliberate practice that determined progression to leadership roles.[196]

We change all the time, even if we don't recognize it. New synapses are formed in our brain with as little as two hours of focused learning.[197] Can you imagine how many you have formed just by reading this book?

Neuroscientists call this 'neuroplasticity': the ability of our brain to form new connections. Brain imaging confirms that new neural paths are created and strengthened through practice, either deliberate (which is when good habits are formed) or unconscious (e.g. when we form a bad habit of checking our smartphone first thing in the morning). We can change the way we process information, and we can change our behaviours and habits.

Evolution demonstrates how animals change behavioural, and even biological, features, based on differences in their environment. They do not choose to change – they adapt. Humans also have an enormous capacity to adapt. But, unlike animals, we decide what, how and how quickly to develop.

ADOPTING THE GROWTH MINDSET

Do you *believe* anyone can change?

A Stanford University professor, Carol Dweck, studied the impact of mindset on capacity to grow and develop. She discovered that people who believe that their qualities are malleable, and can be developed through training and practice, indeed can profoundly change, including flexing their personality.[198]

Dweck called this the 'growth mindset'.

She also described a 'fixed mindset'. This is characterized by a belief that people don't change. Those with a fixed mindset stifle their own growth and the development of others. Multiple studies have yielded the same results: those with a growth mindset learn better,[199] perform better[200] and are more resilient.[201]

As a leader, your primary assumption must be that anyone can grow. Your role is to provide feedback, find the right motivation for development and set expectations to get the best out of people for the benefit of the organization.

And you need to instil this belief in your people. The team needs to feel your belief that they can grow. The balance of expectations, with support, will motivate change and ensure they won't give up half way. So, help them stay on track. Willpower and resilience are the strongest predictors of successful personal transformation.[202]

The result? According to Dweck, those who have this growth mindset are simply better organizational leaders.[203] They turn average workplaces into high-performing organizations.

MAKING BEHAVIOUR CHANGE A HABIT

So, you believe we are capable of growth. How do you intentionally make it happen?

In his best-selling book *The Power of Habit*, Charles Duhigg defined habits as the *choices* that all of us *deliberately* make at some point and then *stop thinking* about but continue doing, often *every day*.[204] The words that stand out here are:

- **Choices**. If we do something at will, then it's up to us if we want to create or change a good or a bad habit.
- **Deliberately**. Habits are not created on a whim but by our conscious actions.
- **Stop thinking**. As actions become automatic, we become unaware of what we are doing – that is, we no longer monitor or see our behaviour... while others do.
- **Every day**. The impact of uncontrolled actions is so significant that, according to studies by researchers at Duke University, up to 40% of our daily actions are not decisions.[205] They are habits. As much as we want to think of ourselves as rational and in control, we are creatures of habit.

Habits may have a bad rap. "This is so habitual of him" or "She has this old habit of..." But, in fact, habits can be a force for good.

Let's imagine that you want to get into a habit of giving feedback. What do you do?

According to research, a behaviour will be performed when:

1. **it is possible** – giving feedback is totally possible;
2. **it is remembered in the moment** – hmm... you may need a reminder;
3. **the preference for its performance is higher than that for any competing behaviour**[206] – what would you possibly want to do instead of giving feedback?

This is a powerful framework that can help us understand how we can build productive habits in ourselves and in our team members.

1. IS IT POSSIBLE?

People learn best through experience or practice. To make an experience *possible*, it must be specific and small.

The good thing about specific and small experiences is that you can practise them. Geoff Colvin talks about the concept of deliberate practice to make acquiring new skills possible. Deliberate practice is something that (1) is specific to practising the skill that you want to acquire, (2) is repetitive, (3) you can get instant feedback on and (4) is not much fun.[207]

Sorry about the "not much fun" part... but, if it were fun, you would probably have the habit already!

2. IS IT REMEMBERED IN THE MOMENT?

The strength of a habit will decrease over time. Unless you practise.

How do you remember to practise? Associate new behaviours with hints and reminders. Those are the situational cues that you create for yourself.

In his book *Triggers*, executive coach Marshall Goldsmith talks about creating reminders and routines that help you stay on the track of meaningful behavioural change. He uses the example of a speed-check display. Those happy faces that appear on a screen when you drive at or below the permitted speed limit – they actually increase good driving behaviours by 30–60%.[208] And this is despite the fact that those are not speed cameras but mere reminders. Checklists and daily routines are simple but powerful tools that can be used to constantly prompt desired behaviours.

3. IS IT PREFERRED?

Duhigg talks about the cue–routine–reward loop by which new habits are formed;[209] when we receive a cue or trigger, it stimulates a set of behaviours or a routine, and the rewards that follow provide the incentive to repeat this cycle whenever a similar cue is received.

We have already established that practising new skills might not be fun. So how do you make it 'preferred', in particular when alternatives exist? How do you ensure the right behaviour is performed? You do it through reward!

Let's use *you*, and the behaviour of giving feedback, as our example. Let's say you see a cue, the poor behaviour of one of your team members. It is negatively impacting their performance and relationship with others. You could do nothing. That is an alternative. But instead, this cue triggers your feedback routine. You give FairTalk feedback. And the reward is immediate! You feel great about yourself; you are honest, straightforward and fair. Your direct report is sincerely thankful and highly motivated to improve. Your leadership credibility soars.

Sound preferable yet?

HONING HABITS THROUGH FEEDBACK

You have adopted the growth mindset. Your team members are full of enthusiasm, trying out new, fledgling behaviours. Now, they need to know whether they are getting it right. Why?

Experience is a great teacher. Not everyone is an equally good learner. We differ in our ability to learn from experience. Your role as a leader is to give feedback, observe the change and then give feedback on progress to ensure that the valuable lessons are extracted.

It should be obvious why feedback on progress is essential. It is entirely possible to practise the wrong behaviour – and practise it until you get good at it!

When we teach development, we tell an anecdote. The story goes that a new manager is given feedback from *his* manager.

"You don't like conflict. You avoid tough conversations. When it comes to the performance of your team, you need to tell it like it is..." The new manager takes the feedback to heart. He also knows that habit is how he will build new skills. And so he decides to give three team members some tough feedback. Every day. For a month. At the end of 30 days he is called into his manager's office and gets fired! "I have to let you go. You have upset the entire team." The new manager exclaims, "But I was just doing what you asked!" His boss replies, "But I didn't tell you to start each conversation with 'Look here, you idiot...'"

Now, in truth, we can't remember whether this story actually happened. Either way, the message is clear. Well-intended people can learn the wrong behaviours just as quickly as they can the right ones.

Leaders often justify not providing this follow-up feedback. With concerning frequency, we hear from leaders phrases such as "Isn't that obvious?" or "But they are senior enough to figure it out." The replies are "maybe" to the first and a definitive "no" to the second.

As it relates to 'being obvious', as we have said, very often our blind spots and biases prevent us from accurately evaluating our own performance.

Relating to seniority, the higher up we get in our careers, the less feedback we get.[210] Without fair information on our performance, we do not know that we need to improve. And the stakes of success or failure increase. Senior leaders need feedback just as much as junior employees. Maybe even more.

Hal Gregersen, executive director of the MIT Leadership Center, talks about how the power and privilege of senior roles insulate some leaders from the truth that they need to hear.[211] Such feedback vacuums have a snowballing effect further down in the organization and create a vicious cycle of chronic feedback deprivation.

FINALLY, DON'T STOP

Sharks are constantly moving. If they didn't they would be dead.

You can apply this analogy to development and growth. Once you have formed a new habit, it's important to keep going. It is all too easy to backpedal into the old behaviours.

Yes, we humans like our comfort. And we define comfort as the condition we are most used to, whether it is the best condition or not.

Perhaps the most well-known example of this is the research on lottery winners who have failed to find ways to enjoy life in their new financial state. Studies have confirmed that, after the initial euphoria, they were not happier than the control group.[212]

So, what can keep us from being drawn back to old comforts? We are most likely to keep moving when we see progress.[213] As a leader, you must provide feedback on how your employees are doing. Your leadership is vital not only in helping others build new habits but also in making sure those take root.

KEY POINTS

Biologically, we are wired to change. We form new synapses when we try new behaviours and reinforce new neural pathways through deliberate practice. A behaviour is performed (practised) when it is possible, remembered in the moment and preferred over the alternatives. Mindset matters greatly for behavioural change to be effective. Those who adopt a growth mindset are more successful at work and in life.

EXPERT'S OPINION

LEADERS LEAD CHANGE ON THE INSIDE

> **Kate Sweetman, founding principal, SweetmanCragun Group**
> Kate is founding principal of SweetmanCragun Group, a global
> leadership development firm. Twice nominated by Thinkers50,
> she is also a former *Harvard Business Review* editor, speaker,
> consultant, mentor and author.

What are the immutable truths of personal change?

When I deal with this question in the classroom, I start with
a joke: a guy buys a hot dog off the cart of a wise zen master.
The guy hands over a $20 bill, gets the hot dog – and nothing
else. "Excuse me," he says politely to the hot dog vendor. "May
I have my change?" "Pardon me, sir," replies the zen hot dog
vendor, very respectfully. "But change comes from within." This
always gets a laugh – and the point is made. It is an ancient and
immutable truth that no one can make someone else change.

Where do you stand on 'nature versus nurture'?

The answer is both! You can't put a fixed number on the per-
centages. Some people come into this world with very strong
characters. They will be who they are almost no matter what.
Others are more sensitive and more subject to influence. Of
course, different young lives are subject to different pressures.
I can speak with some authority. I am the mother of twin girls,
born 90 seconds apart. They were clearly different from each
other from the very start. One is very straightforward and
no-nonsense while the other is a dreamer, filled with empathy
for the world and not very decisive. But they also share traits
that I like to think were instilled by their parents: for example,

they are independent because we gave them opportunities to take independent action.

As a manager, what is my role in the behavioural change of my employees?

People can be led to their own conclusions. This is what enables them to make the internal change necessary to succeed: stop smoking, stop drinking, work harder, collaborate better, take on new skills and new responsibilities – whatever the desired outcome may be. I would argue that the main responsibility of the manager is to create the conditions for employees to understand for themselves their own need to change. The bottom line is this: people change when they are sufficiently dissatisfied with their current state *and* when they internalize that a brighter future awaits them if they change and they can describe what that future is. That realization unmoors them and begins the process of change.

How can we help to sustain change?

Once the euphoria of newness wears off, people realize with dismay the amount of discipline required to keep going in creating new patterns. At that point, they can deeply experience a sense of loss of the familiar, and they tend to revert – their commitment falters. Change takes effort: mental, emotional, social and physical. The role of the leader is to be a coach: to check in with people, tap into where they are and give them that extra boost. A few words of encouragement can make an enormous difference, coming from the right person at the right time in the right way.

PART THREE

FairTalk Culture

Thanks for hanging in with us. Together we've made it through two parts of the book.

Part One dealt with the facts, myths and truths, and principles of feedback – everything you need to know to be a capable leader. Part Two was filled with practical suggestions to increase your effectiveness and capability in giving great feedback. It was about what you need to do.

Part Three is all about culture. Culture is the collective norms and beliefs of a group of people. You, as a leader, define the culture by what you say, do and reinforce. In this part of the book, we will show you how to go beyond individual feedback to create a FairTalk Culture in your team – a culture where fair, focused and credible feedback flows freely in the service of high performance.

How do you create sustainable change and deliver a FairTalk Culture?

The same FairTalk Statement we have already used to change individual behaviour can also be applied to organizational behaviour.

The first part, "Tell me why it matters," is about communication. As a leader, you convey the importance of feedback and its impact on performance. You hold your team accountable for their feedback behaviours. You, and your change management, set the tone.

The second part of the FairTalk Statement is "Tell me how I'm doing." Applied to culture, this means reaching a conclusion about the current state. You need to diagnose current behaviours in your team to pinpoint what needs to change.

Finally, "Tell me what to do differently" becomes all the levers the organization has for supporting sustainable change and for delivering a FairTalk Culture. You pull the levers, such as rewards, structure, technology or other tools, to steer the collective performance in the right direction.

We'll share guidance on the appropriate use of each lever and discuss how to create a FairTalk Culture in your team... even when it isn't supported by the broader company culture.

We recognize that there are particular challenges for leaders operating in contexts that are not especially 'aligned'. And so we also provide a chapter on sustaining the culture you have built and, in particular, on how to do so if the broader environment isn't feedback friendly.

While it may be more challenging, we believe you can build a positive culture within a culture – one that values feedback as a driver of performance. Leaders who build and sustain high-performance environments in the face of resistance build great reputations.

A FairTalk Culture delivers a feedback-rich organization: an organization designed for performance.

EXPERT'S OPINION

CREATING THE RIGHT ENVIRONMENT FOR FEEDBACK

Liz Mellon, chair of the editorial board for
Dialogue Journal, Duke Corporate Education
Liz is a speaker, educator, author and chair of the editorial board for
Dialogue Journal, which reaches a million business readers online
(www.dialoguereview.com). Her thinking spans the hard and soft
aspects of business, as exemplified by some of her best-selling titles,
such as *Inside the Leader's Mind* and *The Strategy of Execution*.[214]

That phrase. "I'd like to give you some feedback."

Watch the hackles rise. Defences go up. The fake smile and "sure" appear. Distrust is deep in our DNA – fear of the new, different and unusual is an inbuilt survival mechanism. We are hard-wired to look for the negatives in life.

Now add to this the idea that we can unwittingly teach children to reject feedback. Children praised for skills and talents prefer tasks they already do well and avoid ones where they may make mistakes. Children praised for *effort* want to challenge themselves, even if they fail at first. They are more likely to succeed in the long term.

Let's add an environment that is hostile to feedback to the mix.

There are many reasons why work can be a dangerous place. Globalization, advances in technology, competition, market disruption... It's an uncertain and unnerving place to inhabit. So we seek success. We believe being perfect or smarter than others is how we get there. This creates a culture of 'I win, you lose'. Actually, everyone ends up losing. And all this before we even get to research that suggests that organizations create environments where psychopaths prosper.[215]

So for feedback to succeed – be heard, acknowledged and acted upon – more than anything else, we need to get the environment right. Given the natural human tendency to avoid feedback, it is absolutely imperative that feedback be expected in the workplace, if not welcomed, and is part of the organizational fabric. We need to create environments where people feel that they matter. Not just a brain to be used, but a whole person to be nurtured.

Step one is to get fear out of the system. If you are afraid of looking foolish, becoming irrelevant or are scared of your boss, your openess to feedback will be diminished.

Nurture a culture that creates Olympic-standard competition. Take any team sport, such as Olympic rowing. There is healthy competition to get on to the team and be the best in the boat. But competition is used to raise the game of the whole team. This can be achieved at work if every employee understands how their work contributes to the organization's purpose, building a focus on the collective prize, not on beating a colleague. Everyone needs to know when and how their contribution makes a positive difference.

And an external focus is critical. If we know what the market and customers want and are aware of our competition, then energy is rightly directed.

Last, and most importantly, we need to develop a culture of learning. It's impossible to change and grow without making mistakes. Mistakes are opportunities to move forward, learn and help others to leapfrog the pitfalls we failed to avoid.

If we could learn even this one lesson it wouldn't only eradicate fear, it would also make work become a lot more fun. And feedback a whole lot easier to give, and to receive.

CHAPTER 12

Tell Me Why It Matters:
Leadership for a FairTalk Culture

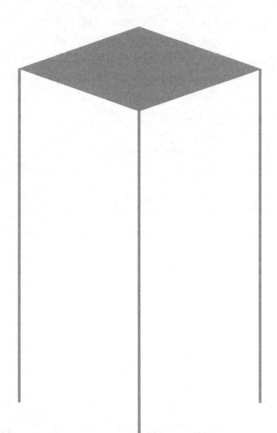

"Accountability is the bridge between what we know is right and what our brains actually want us to do."[216]

Marc Effron, talent consultant

To build a feedback culture, your leadership has to overcome the 'go-to' tendencies that prevent managers from giving feedback. There are myriad reasons leaders give for not doing so. Your role is personal role-modelling, setting the expectations for building a feedback culture, communicating the progress, solid change management and holding your team members accountable.

Sustaining new behaviours is difficult.

More often than not, habit trumps willpower. Only 19% of New Year resolutions last more than two years, and 88% of all resolutions end in failure.[217]

For this reason, many leaders struggle to build a culture of feedback, especially if the sought behaviour runs counter to the broader norms of the organization.

However, when working well, a feedback culture enables individuals to continuously receive, solicit and use formal and informal feedback to improve their job performance. This definition may sound a bit formal but it helpfully points to five important manifestations of a strong feedback culture.[218]

FIVE MANIFESTATIONS OF
A STRONG FEEDBACK CULTURE

RECEIVING FEEDBACK

In feedback-rich cultures, people are receptive to feedback.[219] Soliciting and processing it correctly is actively encouraged. Colleagues provide performance information to each other, even when they are not asked to do so![220]

SEEKING FEEDBACK

In a feedback culture, employees also actively seek feedback. Reasons vary. For some, it is important to have an accurate self-view. For others, it makes completing their tasks easier, as they get timely and useful information on how to do their job better. People new in their role, for example, will be checking in with their supervisor and colleagues particularly often on how well they are doing. Whatever the reason, the science is clear: in environments supportive of feedback, people simply seek more of it.[221]

USING FEEDBACK

This is the ultimate proof of the pudding – utility. Asking others about how you are doing is one thing. But it is not sufficient: feedback-seeking alone will not improve actual performance.[222] That information needs to be put to good use. For performance to improve, the feedback must be internalized and acted upon!

MAKING FEEDBACK BOTH FORMAL AND INFORMAL

Informal check-ins are great. In a feedback culture, leaders have regular, insightful, productive discussions with their employees around how they are doing. But leaders also provide formal feedback. Why do you need formality? A study by CEB Gartner showed that sticking only to informal ways of providing feedback drives the quality of manager–employee conversations down.[223] So, in a feedback culture, the thinking is "Yes, and..." Formal and informal are complementary, not mutually exclusive.

GIVING FEEDBACK CONTINUOUSLY TO IMPROVE PERFORMANCE

Feedback should not be a random managerial act. In particular, in a feedback culture, feedback is timely and frequent. Although we discussed a few situations when immediacy and frequency may be counterproductive (Chapters 1 and 8), in general, the more quality feedback is provided, the better the performance.

TONE AT THE TOP

> *That hackneyed phrase "getting to the top means never having to hear that you're wrong again" needs challenging. Senior leaders should be open to feedback and publicly acknowledge where they are trying to do better. Organizational culture needs careful attention and nurturing, so that work is seen as a place where effort is rewarded, mistakes are treated kindly and people are respected. The right culture doesn't just happen – it needs work.*[224]

Your first obligation is to be a personal role model for the culture you want to build. In very practical terms, this means that you give feedback, frequently, that is fair, focused and credible. You are also open to receiving feedback. You do this because you believe it is the right thing to do. And, if you do nothing else, you have already started to change the culture. Don't believe us?

An average baboon watches its alpha male every 20–30 seconds,[225] because that's where the reward or punishment will come from! Evolution has taught baboons, and us, that watching and imitating the leader's behaviour gets better outcomes.

Outside the wilderness, we keep being professional boss-watchers. That's why organizational cultures are so influenced by the values of those in leadership seats. Employees watch leaders and mirror their behaviours – both the good and the bad.

This means that, as a leader, you are always 'on'. People listen to your every word and observe your every behaviour. They attach meaning to what they see and hear, and create a narrative about who you are and what is important to you.

Larry Summers, President Obama's chief economic adviser, napped for just a moment[226] – and the event infamously became known as "Larry's slumber". Gerald Ratner, CEO of a major jewellery company, made a glib remark at an internal event. He described one of the company's products as "total crap". He cost the organization millions of pounds and ultimately lost his job.[227] Similarly, Lululemon's founder and former CEO Chip Wilson was forced to resign and sell his shares after fat-shaming remarks targeted at his own customers.[228]

Herb Kelleher, on the other hand, is one of the best CEOs (if judged by the many awards he has received and the financial results of his company), not least because of the culture that he created at Southwest Airlines. He tirelessly encouraged his people to have fun at work (himself serving peanuts to passengers) and relentlessly communicated the type of company he wanted Southwest to be.[229] What you say and do matters.

Your positive role-modelling signals what's important.

So, think about your relationship with feedback. What type of feedback do you give? Is it fair and focused? Does it centre around things that matter? Are you truly honest with your employees about their performance? The answers to these questions indicate the type of culture you create.

And, by the way, while your employees are watching you, so too are your peers and your superiors. How do you want to be known?

> *Are leaders in key positions behaving in the ways that we need everyone to behave? Those cultural signals are very potent. It is vital that leaders throughout the organization at all levels understand what they need to know and do.*[230]

COMMUNICATION

Good leaders connect feedback to the business or team strategy. They make the importance of feedback crystal clear.

> In June of 2009, Peter Bregman wrote a thought-provoking piece about culture change on the Harvard Business Review blog network.[231] In his view, changing culture is about changing the stories of an organization. I couldn't agree more. The leader needs to start the process by taking a very visible action that illustrates the new culture – stories will undoubtedly emerge.[232]

How do you connect feedback to team strategy? By showing how feedback creates value as it improves outcomes:
1. Take time to explain how the organization is doing.
2. Show how each group's and each team member's performance contributes to that.
3. Show how others have succeeded because of feedback they received. This strengthens the belief in feedback, so make examples visible.
4. Reinforce how giving feedback 'up, sideways and around' leads to creating value.
5. And then don't ever get tired of making that connection obvious to everyone in the organization.

Providing supporting information will help the employee. A comprehensive description of the business situation and a clear message on what is important has a positive impact on performance. Data from research on US Air Force units prove that employees can use complex, non-linear information when it is included in feedback.[233] And what is a better way to describe the modern workplace than 'complex' and 'non-linear'?

Against the backdrop of the broader environment, zoom in on what is critical, specifically for your team. The FairTalk Statement always starts with *why* a result or behaviour matters. If you do not know what is important, there is no context for an employee to create a mental link between the feedback and the desired result. Use the same structure in your broader communication.

Oh, and you will get an additional benefit: the amount of politics in your group will go down. When employees hear from their managers about what works and what doesn't work in a specific company, their perceptions of politics are reduced, leading to better performance outcomes.[234]

While there are any number of ways you can practically communicate the importance of feedback. Here are four suggestions:

1. Talk with your team about their own beliefs and attitudes towards feedback.
2. Lead a team discussion on personal accountability, as leaders, to provide FairTalk.
3. Take some of the following conversation starters[235] and turn them into a survey. For example, you could ask people whether (and how much) they agree that these statements apply to themselves and the team:
   - Feedback contributes to the success of my employees at work.
   - My feedback can help my employees advance in our company.
   - I find that feedback is critical for my employees to reach their goals.
   - I hold myself accountable for giving feedback to my employees.
   - I feel obliged to follow up on the feedback that I give to my employees.
4. Use the survey results to trigger a discussion with your direct reports or a broader debrief with the team.

In Chapter 14 we will encourage you to make use of metrics to help you stay on track with your culture change efforts. Communicating these metrics to your team provides yet another occasion for talking about the importance of setting expectations and giving clear feedback.

CHANGE MANAGEMENT

It isn't enough to communicate, or even model, a FairTalk Culture. To create a FairTalk Culture, you need to manage the implementation like you would any other major change. Change management, for us, refers to three things:

1. the **result** you want;
2. the **tactics** that will deliver the result;
3. the **hardwiring**, or what you put in place to sustain the change.

To intentionally 'manage change', first you need to understand the *results* you intend to create. In this case, it requires not just that you want 'a FairTalk Culture' but being clear about what that means: a culture where fair, focused and credible feedback flows freely in the service of high performance.

Knowing what drives the desired behaviours enables you to *identify the right tactics* to deliver change. These tactics should be comprehensive. Our view is that culture is an outcome of many factors, all of them interconnected. A change anywhere in the system will be felt everywhere. Tony Richardson and Jock Macneish, in what is still one of the best, most simple analogies, described organizations as 'jelly' – "touch them anywhere, touch them everywhere..."[236]

If our goal is to create a high-performance culture, our tactics must be coordinated and aligned. You can't readily isolate one little bit and fix that without considering its impact on everything else. For example, changing the performance management system may have implications for how rewards are managed. A change in the process may impact roles and responsibilities. An improvement in technology will almost certainly change the process. You must be open to changing anything.

Finally, you need to create 'sticky' change. In other words, you need to *hardwire* your change, monitor progress, course-correct if needed and drive sustainability. Some form of governance will be required to review progress and adjust. This mechanism will also ensure that there are no unintended consequences from the changes you make.

Once you have your change management in place, you can truly implement the final element: holding the team accountable.

HOLDING OTHERS ACCOUNTABLE

Organizations need to value a manager's responsibilities to support people. If a manager isn't providing employees with the information they need to do their jobs and accomplish their goals, the organization should replace them with someone who will.[237]

Your ultimate role, as a leader, is to hold team members accountable for meeting the expectations you have set.

There are two areas where you need to hold high levels of accountability as part of your culture change efforts – not to mention your performance improvement efforts!

First, if you have direct reports who manage others, you must hold them accountable for giving feedback to their employees.

Some say that the best predictor of future behaviour is past behaviour. And they are right. So, if managers do not give feedback today, it is unwise to expect that they will do so in the future. Unless you change the system, set clear expectations and align those with rewards and consequences, nothing will change. You can insist that your direct reports take their people-leadership responsibilities seriously. You can ensure that there are consequences, from those you control, for those who don't give feedback.

Second, you must hold employees accountable to act on the feedback they have been given. New behaviour is a function of consequences. Good leaders make the consequences crisply clear. They also follow up and ensure that consequences happen – both positive and negative.

People will feel compelled to give feedback when the situation does not leave them a lot of choice. Conversely, if left to act in their own self-interest, they will avoid it. There is ample experimental evidence for that. Researchers ran behavioural simulations where people had to distribute money between themselves and an anonymous recipient. In a version of the game where the participant's actions were public, 74% of the participants chose the fair 50/50 option. However, when the transparency was obscured, i.e. the participants were sure they could behave self-interestedly while maintaining the illusion of fairness, the fair 50/50 behaviour dropped to 35%.[238]

In summary, rewarding good behaviours and punishing bad ones drives change. Leading for cultural change is an exercise in instilling accountability.

> *You don't need to convince people to give feedback. You need to dictate, "This is how we think and here is a practical approach." It can (and probably should) be the CEO who sets the course. Amazon's Jeff Bezos wasn't troubled that his team would not like writing six-page memos for meetings. He set expectations. If you've got your organizational leaders in the right place, they will establish the norms.*[239]

> *"This is not an opt-in exercise. Leaders are accountable to give feedback; Employees are accountable to listen and act upon it."*[240]

In short, hold your team accountable.

KEY POINTS

The 'soft' parts of culture are hard. Leaders are responsible for driving a FairTalk Culture. They model the desired behaviours. They are always 'on' and are mindful of their words and actions. They are also feedback advocates. They communicate the value of feedback often and with conviction. They also strive for a feedback culture through rigorous change management that takes a comprehensive perspective on what they aspire to deliver, and how they will deliver and sustain it. Since culture is a composite of many factors, changing one part impacts others so it is important to take a systemic approach to culture shift. Finally, they hold others accountable for behaving consistently with their expectations.

EXPERT'S OPINION

TURNING UP THE DIAL ON FEEDBACK ACCOUNTABILITY

Marc Effron, president, Talent Strategy Group
Marc is president of the Talent Strategy Group and author of the books
8 Steps to High Performance and *One Page Talent Management.*[241]

If you have information that you're convinced will make your company more effective, do you have an obligation to tell your leaders? What if your company has information about you that will help you to be more professionally successful? Would you expect your leaders to tell you? The case to be transparent in these situations may seem obvious until we test that logic on a very easy example – feedback.

The science is clear. Feedback with applied follow-up (not just feedback alone) will help people to improve their skills and behaviours in ways that benefit their careers. If we give others feedback and they accept it, they're more likely be successful. Their feedback to us (if we apply it) will help us be more successful. There's simply no logical case against giving feedback.

The challenge is that the science is equally clear that our brains don't respond well to feedback. They are hard-wired to protect our self-image. When they hear information that doesn't confirm what a great person we are, our brains try to ignore it, refute it or excuse it away. Our brains also don't like conflict, so we hesitate to give feedback to others because we want to maintain the relationships and hierarchies that exist at work.

The consequences – positive or negative – linked to that accountability determine whether we're likely to overcome our natural tendencies and do what's beneficial to us and others. One way to identify whether the consequences are meaningful enough is to use the Accountability Ladder (FIGURE 13).

The Accountability Ladder lists a hierarchy of consequences in increasing order of severity – from barely perceptible to draconian. Each is a consequence of either doing or not doing something. The consequences range from personal knowledge of success or failure to having others know, pay changes, and even to promotion or termination. Each step up the ladder is a meaningful step up from the previous one.

The key question you need to answer is, how beneficial or painful does a consequence have to be before someone takes action? The goal of the Accountability Ladder is to use just enough consequences to create the desired result. If you use too heavy a hand, it's wasteful and can also create a culture of fear if draconian consequences exist for every requested action. Conversely, too light a touch will result in little or no action being taken.

I've found the best level of accountability for giving and seeking feedback is about a 6 (see FIGURE 13). Public knowledge of what others are doing or not doing is a powerful cultural force. It helps to overcome our natural resistance to action. This means you must believe in both accountability *and* transparency – a rare and powerful combination.

The necessary knowledge can be made public by carrying out a simple two-question survey. The first question asks employees whether they have received direct feedback about their performance or behaviours in the past 30 days. The second question asks employees whether their boss has asked for feedback in the past 30 days. Once you have that data, post the raw responses publicly. I can guarantee you that laggards will quickly engage in giving and asking for more feedback.

We can help leaders overcome their hesitancy by creating *just significant enough* incentive for them to do the right thing.

The Accountability Ladder provides a helpful guide to enable you to do exactly that.

FIGURE 13: The Accountability Ladder

CHAPTER 13

Tell Me How I'm Doing:
Diagnosing Your FairTalk Culture

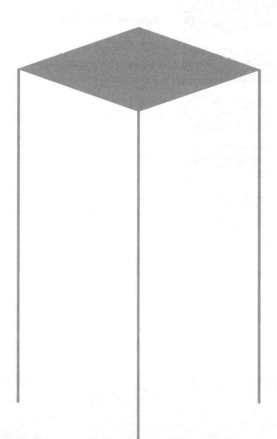

"Organizational structure and systems are incredibly important. Imagine a good kid from a bad neighbourhood who hangs around with the wrong crowd. She goes into juvenile detention. There, she meets a counsellor who helps her to see her own worth, and inspires her to finish her high school degree. But, when her detention is up, she returns to her old neighbourhood: same kids, same school, same everything. How long will her resolve last? Maybe a few days. The same thing happens in organizations. People are behaving in ways that the system encourages. If you want to change behaviours, you also need to change the systems, processes, and relationships that surround the person."**242**

Kate Sweetman, founding principal, SweetmanCragun Group

EVERYONE HAS A FEEDBACK CULTURE... THAT ISN'T THE ISSUE!

The challenge with a feedback culture is not getting one. You have one. The question is whether the one you have is in good enough shape to support peak performance.

To understand whether your feedback culture is enabling,or not, we propose the diagnostic questionnaire in TABLE 7 (next page). It will hclp you to assess the variables that create and define a FairTalk Culture.

Culture is an outcome. As a leader, you have the opportunity to be intentional about the outcome your create. It is determined by the interaction of a series of factors. Any culture is the result of the interplay of these components:
- Structure & Organization;
- Technology & Tools;
- Policy & Process;
- Metrics & Measures;
- Competency & Skills;
- Leadership;
- Change Management.

Consider... does your technology facilitate feedback? Do your policies mandate feedback? Do your people leaders insist on feedback? And so on. You can review how the organizational ecosystem facilitates and reinforces a feedback culture.

Our FairTalk Culture Diagnostic assesses the current state of your culture. It will orient you on the dimension or dimensions of your ecosystem that are likely to work against your efforts.

The diagnostic contains 21 simple statements and asks you to rate your agreement with these statements on a scale of 1 to 5. It is not an exhaustive list of the aspects that could be helpful in assessing whether you have all the right levers in place to drive a FairTalk Culture. However, the statements indicate the types of activity we would expect in a system that drives a feedback culture. As such, the Fair-Talk Culture Diagnostic can provide guidance on where to focus your efforts.

TABLE 7: Cultural differences in giving feedback

CULTURAL LEVER	IN MY TEAM...	SCALE (1 = disagree, 5 = agree)				
	...feedback is required beyond hierarchical relationships or formal teams, such as from internal customers.	1	2	3	4	5
STRUCTURE & ORGANIZATION	...members are expected to receive feedback from, and give feedback to, members of any matrix or cross-functional teams in place.	1	2	3	4	5
	...leaders are required to seek and receive feedback from their team members.	1	2	3	4	5

TECHNOLOGY & TOOLS	...we have tools and technology that facilitate seeking and giving feedback.	1 2 3 4 5
	...the feedback tools are easily accessible and user-friendly.	1 2 3 4 5
	...the tools and technology also help me use the feedback I have received.	1 2 3 4 5
POLICY & PROCESS	...the specifications of what constitutes quality feedback are clearly documented.	1 2 3 4 5
	...there are clear operating instructions on when and how feedback should be given.	1 2 3 4 5
	...the processes of giving and receiving performance feedback are clearly understood by all employees.	1 2 3 4 5
METRICS & MEASURES	...the right feedback actions and behaviours are rewarded.	1 2 3 4 5
	...managers set clear expectations, including goals for what employees need to learn as a result of feedback received.	1 2 3 4 5
	...we have systems in place to track and measure feedback behaviours.	1 2 3 4 5
COMPETENCY & SKILLS	...feedback skills and behaviours are part of a leadership competency model, job profile or job description.	1 2 3 4 5
	...we have the required feedback skills to drive high performance.	1 2 3 4 5
	...we provide adequate time and resources for learning feedback skills.	1 2 3 4 5

LEADERSHIP	...leaders are expected to consistently advocate for the value of feedback.	1	2	3	4	5
	...leaders are expected to set an example by giving high-quality feedback frequently.	1	2	3	4	5
	...leaders are expected to connect feedback to the business strategy and/or the company philosophy.	1	2	3	4	5
CHANGE MANAGEMENT	...we are intentional about changing to a feedback culture and communicate our plans and our progress.	1	2	3	4	5
	...there are robust change management plans that incorporate the tactics we will use across all cultural levers.	1	2	3	4	5
	...we have mechanisms in place to ensure we sustain our progress.	1	2	3	4	5

Simply adding up the scores for each section and comparing them will give you a sense of the relative strengths and weaknesses of each dimension.

FAIRTALK CULTURE DIAGNOSTIC	
CULTURAL LEVER	**TOTAL PER LEVER**
STRUCTURE & ORGANIZATION	
TECHNOLOGY & TOOLS	
POLICY & PROCESS	
METRICS & MEASURES	
COMPETENCY & SKILLS	
LEADERSHIP	
CHANGE MANAGEMENT	

The next chapter gives practical ideas on improving the cultural ecosystem and delivering a sustainable feedback culture. You will learn how to address those lower-scoring culture drivers and how to strengthen or sustain higher-scoring drivers.

NOW WHAT?

There are three considerations for taking this diagnostic forward.

1. KNOW THE BASELINE

Your choice of tactics will depend on where you are starting from. If the prevailing culture is open and candid, you may be able to rely less on structured, formal processes. If the culture is not open, then you may need to implement structured processes, start with training or introduce systems of accountability. Be thoughtful.

2. TEST THE READINESS

You know the current culture. You know what is most likely to work and what is most likely to be rejected out of hand. The diagnostic will help you identify all the areas of opportunity. But you need to decide from those opportunities which are the right levers to focus on. You must balance the changes that will most move your group forward with the realities of the prevailing culture.

How will you find the right balance? Ask. Involve team members. Involve your HR department. Involve your own manager. Involve peers. Your non-negotiable is that you intend to create a culture of feedback (you might call it something different), but let others know you'd like their perspective on how best to move forward.

3. SELECT OPPORTUNITIES

Now you know your baseline. You have selected areas of focus. You next need to determine solutions that will really work. Ignoring this vital context risks diminishing feedback and, ultimately, performance. You need to avoid changes based on current external trends or fads and ones that don't take account of the specifics of your team and organization.

KEY POINTS

To drive performance further, you will want to create a culture that consistently and frequently delivers high-quality feedback. Because culture manifests itself as commonly accepted behaviours, it is visible and can be measured. The FairTalk Culture Diagnostic describes the components needed to deliver an organization with a FairTalk Culture. To move forward, you can use the diagnostic to assess the baseline culture, identify key drivers, engage stakeholders in your change management plans and select opportunities to affect change.

EXPERT'S OPINION

WHAT AM I UP AGAINST?

Alan L. Colquitt, author and research scientist,
Center for Effective Organizations
Alan is an independent consultant, adviser and author on a variety of
topics in the field of organizational behaviour. His latest book,
Next Generation Performance Management,[243] challenges the
common assumptions and misconceptions of how people
perform in organizations.

Why is there a lack of feedback culture in organizations?

Feedback in organizations is typically a formal part of a performance management process, the sole purpose of which is to evaluate performance to differentiate rewards. And, most importantly, only top-scoring employees get the big rewards. Supervisors know most of their people will be disappointed. This makes it hard to get excited about giving feedback.

This dynamic leads to four fundamental problems that result in feedback scarcity in most organizations:

1. Employees are not happy with the information they are getting on their performance. They may not be getting any feedback. In other cases the feedback simply isn't very useful or, worse, it is actually damaging to performance.

2. Next, managers don't enjoy delivering messages to employees. Their job as a manager is to tell their employee that their performance isn't cutting it and they need to get back on track. Rather than acting as coaches, supervisors are acting as judges and focusing on what employees are doing wrong.

3. Also, managers have little incentive. They have individual work to do in addition to their supervisory responsibilities.

They are typically rewarded for the quality of their individual work, not the quality of their supervisory work. The best people managers are rarely adored by their organizations. In organizations, we adore the 'producers', not the 'coaches'.

4. Finally, many managers simply aren't skilled at giving feedback. The problem with feedback is a framing problem. One of the important lessons from research is that people need feedback on *progress*. It isn't feedback that is motivating to employees, per se, it is *progress*. This takes real practice and real training. Most organizations don't invest enough in these programmes. We would have more success with managers if we reframed their responsibility from 'giving feedback on performance' to 'ensuring progress on the things that matter through feedback'.

What organizational support do managers need to build a culture of feedback?

Most organizations simply don't provide the resources managers need. They provide administrative resources, such as job aides, to handle the mechanics, but they don't provide enough resources on *how* to provide the feedback the employees need.

Take advantage of all of the feedback, coaching and interpersonal skills training the organization provides. These skills form the bedrock for building feedback competence.

Find your own resources if the organization doesn't provide them. There are many good books and public training programmes available on feedback.

So, if managers don't give feedback, what is your advice to employees?

I think we over-rely on managers to provide feedback. If the dominant model in organizations views feedback as evaluative, this puts the supervisor in the centre since they do the evaluating. It is really only their perspective that counts. But employees need to feel empowered to get the information they need on their own if their supervisor isn't providing it.

CHAPTER 14

Tell Me What to Do:
Practical Ways to Build
a FairTalk Culture

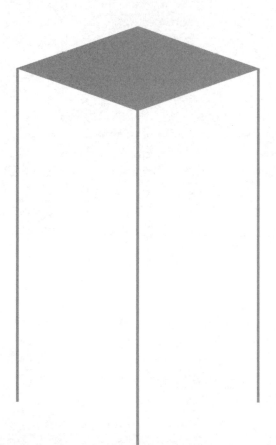

"Give us the tools, and we will finish the job."[244]

Winston Churchill, politician

In this chapter, we provide practical advice on how, as a leader, you can build on your individual excellence as a feedback giver to create a FairTalk Culture.

In Chapter 13, you used the FairTalk Culture Diagnostic to understand your current culture of feedback. Applied properly, each of the seven components or levers – Structure & Organization, Technology & Tools, Policy & Process, Metrics & Measures, Competency & Skills, Leadership and Change Management – has the potential to boost your FairTalk Culture. You already learned about two of those, Leadership and Change Management, in Chapter 12. Now, we will walk you through the rest.

GOOD POLICY

We have talked about all the reasons why managers don't give feedback. That won't change unless there is a clear expectation. Transparent expectations, through explicit policy, for what is appropriate (or not) are important considerations in building a feedback culture.

At a minimum, your policy should specify the transparent expectation for regular, ongoing informal feedback and a minimum frequency for formal feedback. In general, you want your feedback to happen shortly after you've observed an opportunity for performance improvement, and you want it to be reasonably frequent.[245] How frequent? It does not have to be as often as you think.

In a study of safety behaviours at an industrial plant, researchers found that a combination of training, goal setting and feedback increased safety performance from 65% to 96%.

But the truly interesting insight was that there was no significant difference between providing feedback once a week or twice a week.[246] As mentioned earlier, feedback delivered too often may reduce both learning and task performance.[247]

Beyond the 'minimum', what we would consider a *strong* policy is one that:

- *reduces variability* in approach;
- builds in *quality*.

Why should you want to reduce *variability*? Variability allows for individual interpretations by managers of what 'good' might look like. W=However, previously we established in Chapter 1 that the beliefs of managers can sometimes be misguided and lead to erroneous behaviours.

Allowing too much variability may also result in conflicting approaches. Where there is inconsistency, managers get confused and revert to the good old status quo – do nothing. Inconsistency also diffuses accountability. It's easier to hide when it wasn't clear what was expected.

Too much variability also means employees don't know what to expect – which isn't transparent. It also makes it difficult for employees to demand feedback from their leaders.

Good policy also builds in *quality* by requiring three things.

I. ADJUSTMENT FOR CONTEXT

When assessing performance, good policy both permits and requires managers to take context into account. They should consider the complexity of the operating environment, the adversity of the situation, and the support that has or has not been provided to help a person attain their goals. We called these 'feedback modifiers' in Chapter 4. They complicate the job of delivering accurate and useful feedback but increase the accuracy of the feedback and the chances that it will be acted upon.

2. FOCUS ON PERFORMANCE FIRST, DEVELOPMENT SECOND

Good policy makes clear that performance comes first and development second.

Often managers avoid difficult conversations about performance today, preferring to turn them into easier conversations about what employees need to change to be more effective later in their careers. If you set your policy to focus on performance, employees will act more quickly and with more zeal than when they are merely given a personal development target.[248]

In our view, there is also an integrity aspect to this. Focusing on career or long-term development without addressing performance issues relevant to the current role is, at the very least, irresponsible. Lacking valuable feedback needed to improve today jeopardizes future success.

Making it 'all about performance' can support a virtuous cycle. When employees are appropriately challenged with work tasks, the natural outcome is for them to ask for more information on their performance to make it easier. However, if the stretch they are asked to make is too small, they won't bother asking how they are doing. Similarly, turn the heat up too much and they will be overwhelmed. Performing in the zone with the right amount of pressure naturally urges employees to seek more feedback.[249]

Focusing on performance also places the emphasis on the task, not the individual. This makes it easier to reduce negative reactions and defensiveness. For instance, data from experiments at the University of California, Los Angeles, suggest that when information directly affects our self-opinion, the feedback is more likely to be misinterpreted.[250] So a quality policy emphasizes feedback on tasks.

Performance (versus development) conversations do not need to be hard. Just apply the FairTalk Statement.

3. DIVERSIFY SOURCES OF FEEDBACK

A good policy also recognizes that there will be cases when a manager's credibility will be low and their subordinates will be likely to discard the manager's feedback. To manage this, good policy requires that feedback to the employee come from a range of sources.

Chapter 6 covers the variety of sources that can increase the accuracy and credibility of feedback.

While the policy must never remove the manager's accountability for applying judgement in providing feedback, it should consider a variety of sources. Some organizations will also empower employees to solicit additional feedback – for example, crowdsourced feedback may increase the credibility of the message.

STRONG PROCESSES

Good policy is supported by strong processes. A strong process is one that embeds the policy requirements discussed above into a set of procedures, thereby delivering the principles of good feedback – fairness, focus and credibility.

Good processes also make roles and responsibilities clear. Chapter 5 (see TABLE 3) lays out the reasons why managers don't give feedback. One reason is that they don't consider it to be a part of their job. Clearly, this is the result of a process failure in assigning and ensuring accountability to the manager for driving performance.

Getting more sophisticated, a smart process flow can be sequenced to 'prime' leaders to look for bias in their own thinking. Consider designing the process's steps to include reminders on potential bias, at the time of decision making, to increase accuracy. Daniel Kahneman nicely sums up why this is helpful: "Our thoughts and our behaviour are influenced, much more than we know or want, by the environment of the moment."[251] Even a single slide in a presentation, a poster on the wall in the performance calibration meeting or a pop-up window at the right time in the process will result in fairer diagnosis. And fairer diagnosis means more accurate feedback and, ultimately, improved performance.

A good process can also do more than prime decision makers. It can reduce the risk of bias in two practical ways:

- Using a structured approach to collect employees' inputs helps to minimize social and cognitive biases.
- Independent data collection, prior to sharing, reduces the risk of respondents' opinions being influenced by others.

To achieve reliability, leaders insist on clear processes, focus on process improvement and review the process if outcomes are below expectations. They then insist on the process being applied consistently, over time.

METRICS & MEASURES

Policy sets expectations. Processes support execution. But it is metrics and measures that deliver accountability.

The value of measures in behavioural change should not be underestimated. Jeffrey Pfeffer, from Stanford University, takes a firm stand:

Unless and until leaders are measured for what they really do and for actual workplace conditions, and until these leaders are held accountable for improving both their own behaviour and, as a consequence, workplace outcomes, nothing will change.[252]

Metrics contribute to a FairTalk Culture by gauging whether feedback is actually happening. KPIs on the number of employees with performance goals, on whether formal feedback conversations have occurred, on employee satisfaction with feedback, etc. – all these are examples of metrics and measures that can act as mechanisms for leaders to hold a high level of accountability.

If you want to move beyond measuring feedback provision, you could think about including KPIs on the outcomes of feedback – for example, has the employee's performance improved? Has there been a visible change in behaviours? Are the team's results going up? On the basis of 'what gets measured gets done', metrics can act as a catalyst, until such a time as the culture of feedback is deeply embedded.

When we talk about measures, some think that it is all about dashboards and big data. Not at all. It can be as easy as providing 'sad face' and 'smiling face' buttons for people to push at the entrance to the canteen to react to a question such as "Are you happy with the quantity of feedback you received today?"

STRUCTURE & ORGANIZATION

When it comes to feedback, considerations of organization structure are important. As a leader, keep asking yourself, "Is my organizational structure making feedback easier?"

Let's start with the team that you manage. Consider, for example, the span of control. Span of control is the number of direct reports each manager has. If there are too many direct reports, the time available to each for dedicated feedback and coaching will be reduced. Unfortunately, this is the current trend. Bosses now manage, on average, nine direct reports, up from five in 2008 according to Gartner, which can spread leaders so thinly that they don't have a close grasp of what their employees are doing. "Managers are less likely to provide good feedback and coaching when they don't understand what that employee's workflow is," says Brian Kropp, HR practice leader at Gartner.[253]

Further, the more reports, the greater the logistical challenges of feedback. Research confirms that the more direct reports you have, the less likely they are to ask you for feedback.[254]

Then there is what happens beyond your own immediate structure.

In complex environments, matrix structures are typically employed to get work done. For example, an employee may report to a business unit but also report to a technical function. Another example may be reporting functionally but also geographically.

If your environment has any or all of these configurations, performance requires that feedback happens within the direct hierarchical structure as well as the matrix structure. There are two aspects:

- giving feedback *across* the matrix;
- collecting inputs for feedback *from* the matrix.

Leaders looking to build a culture of feedback put in place approaches to ensure feedback takes account of the mosaic (or an abstract painting, sometimes, where the ear is positioned next to the belly button!) that is today's organizational structure.

Collecting feedback across and from the matrix partners can be easier than you think. An effective way of gathering feedback about your employees from the matrix is to send the key stakeholders a small number of uncomplicated questions related to their interactions with your team members.

It can be as straightforward as the following example:

Hi Angela!
I am collecting feedback for Sergey so I can give him specific guidance on how to improve his literary prowess. Over the past few months, he has been working with you on an excellent book. I trust you had numerous opportunities to observe his penmanship and collaborative behaviours first-hand. I would like you to share those observations with me. There are only three short questions:
What should Sergey…

START DOING	
STOP DOING	
CONTINUE DOING	

Please be specific and, if possible, provide examples of situations where you saw the behaviour. I will anonymize all the feedback before sharing it with him.

Thanks a lot,
The Editor

This basic approach would give Angela a lot of scope for giving powerful feedback, simply.

Giving the feedback provider a week or two to respond is good practice. Be mindful of the number of people you are asking – this is a request for their time. Getting three to five points of view is typically sufficient. Check Chapter 6 for ideas on whom you may want to ask.

And remember that the term 'matrix structure' is not just used to describe formal, dual reporting relationships. Increasingly, it describes the multiple cross-functional teams (with or without formal reporting) that are so critical to getting work done. Swarms, project teams, leaderless teams, tiger teams, scrums, modular task groups... pick your favourite term. In the absence of formal responsibility for giving feedback, you must implement alternative approaches.

A further, and common, informal relationship is that of the internal customer. In the case of a team that provides services to other parts of the business, the leader can easily set up mechanisms to gather customer feedback. A simple solution would be to ask for feedback on individual team members, using the same template you used to solicit feedback from matrix or cross-functional partners.

An alternative is to consider gathering 'collective feedback'. This is feedback on the performance of the group, rather than the individuals in it. It can be identified by asking people to complete a survey, or it could be more qualitative, for example collected from a focus group. In this case you would assemble it for the express purpose of sharing feedback about the performance of the team.

You can use collective feedback to improve team performance or take this generalized feedback and make it specific to the individual members of your team.

Finally, so far we have been focusing on collecting feedback. But you can also *give* feedback to colleagues who form part of the formal or informal organizational structure. As indicated in the previous chapter, you will decide how ready the culture is for that. But, if you can do it, you have the perfect tool. The three-part FairTalk Statement from Chapter 7 can be used to give feedback within the informal structure: explain the importance of an issue, share observations on the progress and the current status, and make clear what you would expect to see done differently.

TECHNOLOGY & TOOLS

Do you have the right tools to support feedback? These should relate to both giving and receiving. The right technology? These factors impact the ease, or otherwise, of feedback.

Whatever the answers, a good place to start is with the *why*. Technological solutions may be appealing in their novelty – just make sure that you ground yourself in the right reasons for choosing tools and technology that are designed to facilitate feedback.

There are many such tools and they vary greatly in their uses, sophistication, format, design, etc. We group them by their purpose in TABLE 8, and the following sections provide more detail.

TABLE 8: Feedback tools

PURPOSE OF THE TOOL	EXAMPLES
OFFICIAL RECORDS OF PERFORMANCE	Performance evaluations, talent review systems
TOOLS FOR COLLECTING FEEDBACK	Multi-rater 360-degree surveys, crowdsourced feedback, customer feedback forms
'HOW-TO' TOOLS	Guides, training courses, performance support
COMMUNICATION SUPPORT	Posters, emails, videos

OFFICIAL RECORD OF PERFORMANCE

It is very likely that you already have an official 'system of record' in your organization. Typically, this is technology that stores feedback data, such as performance evaluations. It is a single point of reference for historical performance feedback from you and other colleagues about employees.

Although many managers dislike the task of writing performance evaluations, there are some undeniable benefits:

- It forces you to prepare.
- It makes you focus on the essential.
- Having feedback recorded and shared with employees in writing increases their accountability to act on it.
- Your feedback is available to other people in the organization who can help your employees with their development.
- While we would prefer this not to be needed, it does provide documented proof that feedback was given, in the case of dispute.

When written performance evaluation is a standard practice in your organization, your responsibility as a leader is to create expectations that all managers do it, and do it well.

TOOLS FOR COLLECTING FEEDBACK

Recently, even some established systems of record have made moves to make it easier to give and receive feedback. Some of them have built-in functionalities to collect multi-rater feedback, the most common examples being online 360-degree feedback (collected from self, boss, direct reports, peers and customers), 180-degree feedback (self, boss and direct reports) and upward feedback (direct reports only). There are also multiple stand-alone solutions of various degrees of complexity.

Additionally, there are smaller fit-for-purpose apps that crowdsource real-time feedback from colleagues. Many large organizations adopt these. They can be particularly effective in project-based and leaderless environments. If you work for a small company that cannot afford an expensive system, these agile self-service tools can do a superb job of collecting feedback from multiple sources in a fun and engaging way.

'HOW-TO' TOOLS

When we speak about feedback tools, we do not necessarily mean technology. Your employees and their managers need support to give and receive feedback well. You can make available and promote the use of 'how-to' support tools such as training courses, manager guides, instructional videos or mobile apps that provide just-in-time guidance. Increasingly, managers value in-the-moment support more than formal training.

COMMUNICATION SUPPORT

These tools enable change management. Posters, emails, videos, visual reminders – these are all ways you can communicate your leadership expectations around giving feedback. You are only limited by your (and your team's) creativity.

WHICH ONES TO CHOOSE?

It can be challenging to choose exactly what you need. Alignment with your structure, consistency with your process and potentially configuration with other systems will be some of the considerations affecting your decision. These can be big issues. But the most important of the seven components is Leadership. Low-tech solutions, such as our start/stop/continue tool for collecting individual feedback or the focus group approach to collective feedback we shared above, can be just as powerful as high-tech solutions when there is strong leadership. Similarly, the best high-tech solutions, without leadership, will surely fail.

The leader's role is to be clear on the purpose of the tools, to promote fairness in using them and to ensure that the outcome (delivered feedback) improves performance. Ideally, you should have support tools from each category: a system of record, feedback collection tools, how-to tools and communication support. But deciding exactly what you will have, and how much, is your discretion and responsibility.

One final consideration. Ensure the tools you use do not take accountability away from the manager. Technology should not be a crutch. It may be tempting to crowdsource feedback all the time. But it is ultimately the role of the manager to align the improvement opportunity with the organization's goals and deliver a focused message in a way that makes the employee care.

COMPETENCY & SKILLS

Policy and process, and even good leadership, aren't enough if there isn't also capability to execute.

> *Clients will often do specific training around their process. We are called when the approach does not work and there is actually a need to build mindset and capability in addition to the new process.*[255]

To build the feedback capabilities of others in your organization, you need to ensure that your managers have access to the right knowledge, skills and beliefs about feedback through the relevant reading (this book is a good start) and training. Make sure they apply those skills to work.

> *The path to success involves intentionally practising these important leadership behaviours day to day until they become fully integrated with work.*[256]

MAKE EVERYONE CONSCIOUS
OF UNCONSCIOUS BIAS

As we said in Chapter 6, ensuring feedback is fair means checking for unconscious bias. You need to be aware of unconscious bias. You also need to be aware that recent research casts doubt on the value of training people to avoid their unconscious bias.[257] (Although this does not mean that you should not strive to increase awareness of it.)

In a feedback culture, leaders are educated on bias and there is a clear expectation that leaders will actively work to reduce biases. Systems for aligning feedback (Chapter 6) help with this, as do third-party reviews of assessments (of course, you are more diligent when someone is likely to check up on your work). While it is impossible to get rid of bias, leader awareness and conscious checking against the most pertinent forms of social (gender, age, race) and cognitive bias will enhance fair feedback. Making people aware of their biases, training and just-in-time priming (providing reminders to be aware of our own tendencies to succumb to bias) are ways to help managers make better decisions.

EDUCATE MANAGERS IN THE FAIRTALK MODEL

Providing managers with a structure to deliver useful and fair feedback will help to build their skills.

Frameworks and models, consistently applied, bring about competence, goodwill and trustworthiness. Our three-step FairTalk Statement is easy to teach and can be used in any situation when a person needs to provide feedback. And it is proven that people are more willing to give feedback in workplaces that value learning and development.[258]

You can build skills with a good framework and through practice, but building real capability is quicker when it is also accompanied by observation and reflection. As your team members practise new skills, take the opportunity to have individual conversations about their experiences, coach them where needed, and recognize and reward their success.

HIRE OR PROMOTE WITH FEEDBACK IN MIND

Once you understand the importance of feedback, it becomes clear that considering feedback skills (along with other things) when assessing the quality of team members is just good sense. You can promote internally, or hire from outside, with feedback skills in mind. And you should... if you care about performance.

While it is harder to assess the presence of these skills in candidates you don't know, it is possible to get insights. You can use personality tests and/or competency-based interview questions to examine candidates' likely approach to giving feedback.

When it comes to personalities, some people are just more innately wired to be good at giving feedback that supports performance. Personalities that are predisposed to help others tend to create an environment conducive to personal growth and development. People who are conscientious and dependable will typically adhere to the organizational policies and processes you put in place. And individuals who are more naturally curious receive more feedback.[259]

Conversely, highly socially sensitive individuals may not confront problems, or they may wish to avoid confrontations. They may be less willing to provide feedback.

We can all learn to give great feedback but there is no doubt that, if you are wired for it, you will find it easier. Even if you have promoted someone to a supervisory role who does not have the personality predispositions to give feedback, it is not a problem. Just set very clear expectations and build their skills.

But let's return to the hiring process. Either in place of or in addition to personality assessment, you can use interview questions to better understand whether you are hiring a leader who is good at feedback.

The gold standard for interview questions is 'behavioural' questions. These questions focus on what a candidate has *done*. As an interviewer, you pose questions that give you insight into a situation and have the candidate explain, with great specificity, what they actually did – that is, how they behaved. You then explore the results or outcomes they achieved.

So, what would be good behavioural questions? You could start with: "Could you tell me about a time you gave tough feedback to a subordinate? What was the situation? Then, please tell me very specifically what you said and did."

Now sit back and listen hard! Finally, when you have a very detailed picture of the candidate's behaviour, ask, "And what was the outcome?"

The answer to this question lets you assess all sorts of things. For example, what triggered the person to actually give feedback? How do they define 'tough'? Did they prepare before giving the feedback? What did they say and how did the receiver react? Did the receiver understand the feedback and improve as a result? Did the manager follow up? And so on.

(If you want to be cheeky, you could even ask the candidate to give you in-the-moment feedback on your recruitment process, as they have experienced it so far. For example, "Give me some helpful feedback on our interview process today.")

There is one question you should not ask! Don't ask, "How good are you at giving feedback?"

First, the candidate may mislead you. And you already know the second reason!

We have said from the outset that a fundamental challenge with feedback is that we all suffer from low self-awareness and don't assess our own abilities accurately. Therefore, even a candidate who doesn't intentionally try to manage your impression is unlikely to answer accurately.

So, ask great questions. And hire as part of building a feedback culture among your other considerations.

As you can see, there are many levers that can be deployed to build a feedback culture. You can select some or all of these simple tactics. The good news is that you have established a baseline by performing the FairTalk Culture Diagnostic in Chapter 13. The areas where you identified the biggest opportunities can inform your strategy.

KEY POINTS

Building a feedback culture requires the creation of an ecosystem made up of elements that explicitly, or more subtly, promote feedback. Good policy makes leadership expectations for feedback behaviours clear and prominent. Strong processes ensure execution of the policy. Measures and metrics create accountability and allow progress to be tracked. Recognizing the nature of organizational structures allows feedback to be collected from all the sources that can observe and help to improve performance. Supporting tools can assist with collecting and recording feedback and can help to instruct managers and communicate expectations. Leaders must choose tools that match their organization and their specific needs. Building individual feedback skills also contributes to the overall organizational capability. And, whether you are promoting from within or hiring from outside, considering a candidate's skills and beliefs around feedback will contribute to building a FairTalk Culture.

EXPERT'S OPINION

BUILDING FEEDBACK-CAPABLE ORGANIZATIONS

Rob Sheppard, vice president, BTS and VanDyck Silveira,
managing director, BTS
Rob has worked with over 2,000 leaders across the world over the
course of his more than 20-year career in leadership development.
VanDyck successfully led client engagement efforts with such executive
education industry leaders as Duke Corporate Education, the Financial
Times and IE Business School's Corporate Learning Alliance, and BTS.

What does it take to teach someone how to give effective feedback?

Years ago, we used to teach specific skills, such as project management or timekeeping. Alas, the typical scenario was that we would teach and there would be improvement... followed by the person slipping back into old behaviours.

So, today, we teach skills in context. Leaders need to give feedback and make sure that it's heard and acted upon. And the process is not always linear. So we teach feedback principles, situational awareness, dealing with emotions... and it takes a concerted effort.

But teaching feedback is only as effective as the degree to which those skills get used. Beyond 'teaching', setting the tone is critical. It comes down to managerial accountability, and this is where we also need to work with the need to shift a person's mindset. That is really hard.

What works best with teaching feedback skills?

Managers increasingly ask for something personalized: how will it work in specific cases related to them? They appreciate the performance context more and more. In response, we use new methods to teach feedback, such as 'surgeries'. People come with real cases and we bring them to life to debrief and extract lessons.

It is important to focus on behaviours, not attitudes. We work a lot with examples. What people often miss out is the impact of their behaviours, and real-life examples help with positioning and illustrating that.

Simulations and action learning are becoming extremely popular. This is an approach that we recently took with a global bank. In the programme, which is centred around participants working as a team and running a bank over a number of trading cycles, we provide observation and team and individual feedback. Over the course of the programme, we transfer the ownership of feedback from us to the participants, which mirrors the client's expectations. One thing that really helps is that the bank's behavioural code is extremely clear and well constructed, and for this reason it is powerful. Therefore, using such a behavioural code makes people's lives simpler and feedback much more likely.

Are you seeing an increase or decrease in demand for courses on feedback?

It is not about more or less – it's always been there. But today there is more demand for feedback and difficult conversations at more senior levels of the organization, not only for frontline leaders. Top-level leaders think they know the stuff, but they are not doing it, so we need to engineer this to happen. And sometimes we have to deal with some resistance from HR. For example, working with the board of a major mining company, we were told, "You will struggle to get the leaders' full attention." In reality we had two hours of exciting conversations. The leaders were all engaged and stepped up to lead the cultural transformation.

CHAPTER 15

Making the
FairTalk Culture
Sustainable

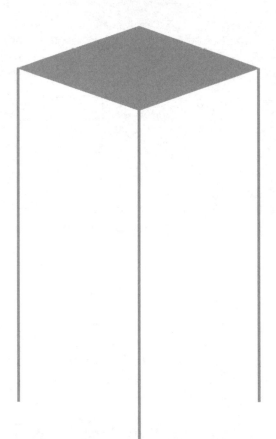

"The factors that affect feedback are mostly to do with good technique, a hunger to always do better and an open and curious learning environment."[260]

Ellen Maag, partner at Heidrick & Struggles

You are done!

If you are following our guidance, you are not only giving feedback but you're also activating the levers that will deliver a high-performing environment that thrives on feedback.

But, as a leader, you are unlikely to feel you have finished. In fact, you are likely to conclude that you never 'arrive'. Indeed, you can always strive to continuously improve the culture of fairness and transparency in the teams you lead.

So, let's fast-forward 12 months. How are the changes working for you?

If you have planned well and been diligent, you should be seeing some positive results: performance improvement, better behaviours, greater motivation, etc. But the chances are that you have aspects you want to improve, or results that you're still not happy about. And this may have nothing to do with you. Organizations are dynamic. It is impossible for you to control everything. You need to continually gauge what's going on, and adjust.

So, this chapter is our troubleshooting manual for a FairTalk Culture.

TROUBLESHOOTING YOUR CULTURE

We believe it is possible to identify common problems with sustaining a feedback culture within teams and organizations. Just like any good how-to manual, this section does exactly that.

Good leaders are also good doctors. For your team or organization, you need to be able to observe the symptoms, make an accurate diagnosis and prescribe the right treatment:

- **Symptoms** are the metrics or behaviours that you might observe. They indicate that something is not 100% okay.
- **Diagnosis** is your judgement of the situation. You will want to get it right, as it will determine the subsequent interventions.
- **Treatment** is the course of action you take to course-correct your culture.

In essence, the troubleshooting decision tree shown in FIGURE 14 is a summary of what we have discussed so far. Refer to it when the feedback or performance improvement cycle isn't working. This practical tool directs you to the specific action needed, based on your diagnosis.

THE TROUBLE WITH TROUBLESHOOTING IS… ABSOLUTELY NOTHING

Culture is complex and takes time to build. Getting it right first time is theoretically possible, just not very probable!

One thing that can make delivering this culture especially hard is when the cultural aspirations you have for the team run counter to the prevailing organizational culture. If the broader organizational culture is allergic to feedback, your task will simply be a slower build.

That said, it is still possible to build that culture of open feedback. You just have to be prepared to go 'countercultural'.

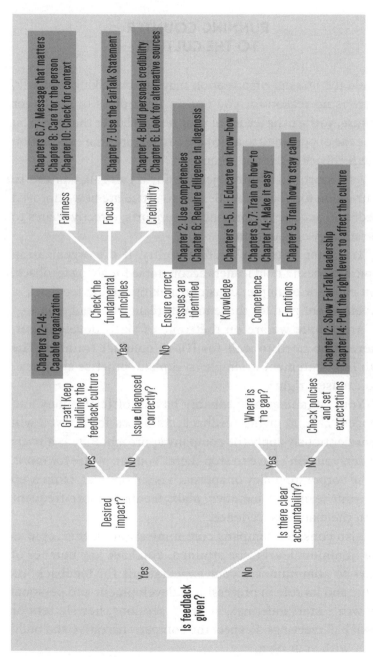

FIGURE 14: FairTalk Culture troubleshooting decision tree

RUNNING COUNTER
TO THE CULTURE

While the broader organization may not be talking feedback, there is no reason for you not to. Regardless of the larger culture, you are the leader of your team. You set the tone. You have the opportunity to articulate to the team your expectation that feedback is fair and frequent.

As a start, link your objective for a FairTalk Culture to your vision for your team. Be able to articulate how improved feedback, and the performance it supports, directly relates to the strategy of your team.

The same is true of accountability. If the organization typically doesn't hold leaders accountable for giving feedback, you can. For example, consider making 'giving feedback' a development goal for those in your team who lead others.

And, while we are on the topic of skills development, there is no need to wait for HR to conduct training. The FairTalk Statement is simple to explain, practise and learn. No excuses, right?

Your organization probably has an official policy and process around giving feedback. As a *good* leader, you will conscientiously apply the company approach. But, as a *smart* leader, you don't have to stop there. You can aspire for more. If the corporate policy or approach is suboptimal, ramp it up for your team. For instance, make feedback more frequent than the mandated cadence.

Also consider company communication on this topic as the minimum level to be attained. You have any number of ways to communicate your expectations for feedback, its value and its role in professional development and personal growth – staff meetings, strategy sessions, newsletters or town hall meetings. Respect the company narrative and build on it with your own.

As a leader, you probably have the final say in recruiting for your team. Hiring and promoting those who take and give feedback well is a decision that sits with you for those you manage.

When you go countercultural, another simple step you can take is to set up basic metrics. You can track what you or your managers do, for example, by tracking how often formal feedback is given. You can track how the feedback is received by asking employees. And you can even monitor the topics of the feedback and listen for the trends.

Leaders continuously troubleshoot in order to achieve a high-performance environment. A good leader looks for opportunities to double down, or adjust, or sometimes redo. What they are actually doing is creating sustainability.

The biggest risk to success may not be that culture is hard to change. Or even that it can be fragile if we make the wrong move. The biggest risk is that leaders do not stay the course. So stay the course!

And, if you do, you will reap the benefits.

KEY POINTS

Building and sustaining a high-performance culture is challenging and requires constant work. Leaders need to be mindful of the observable symptoms so that they can correctly diagnose the issues that undermine or hamper their culture-building efforts. When leaders address the feedback culture, as well as addressing individual performance, they create a unique blend of people, behaviours, processes, structures, systems and measures that collectively drive high performance. When the wider organization is not conducive to feedback, going countercultural is taking leadership responsibility for creating an environment that delivers great results.

EXPERT'S OPINION

CULTURE CHANGE

Jeff Anderson, president and CEO,
Lake Forest Graduate School of Management
Jeff is the president and CEO of Lake Forest Graduate School of
Management, a revolutionary business school that uses a faculty
composed entirely of senior business leaders. Throughout his career
as a business leader, adviser to senior executives and educator,
Jeff has brought unique and powerfully effective insights to
the practice of leadership.

I've had the pleasure of working with senior executives for almost 20 years. I haven't met one who wasn't committed to changing the culture of their organization. Yet very few succeed in a sustainable way. Why? The points of failure are all too common:

- They don't have a good grasp of the current culture and how or why it came to be. How can you focus your efforts around something you don't understand?
- The change effort is outsourced to a steering committee, a project team with a fancy name or HR. It becomes one more thing to manage and oversee, essentially a spectator sport.
- Leaders get bored and distracted. The pressure to see a quick impact works against the patient, focused effort needed to change a culture. It takes years.
- Leaders don't put enough emphasis on building disciples – individuals who share the vision and embody the new behaviours.

- Leaders move too slowly to address people in powerful positions who are resisting or undermining the effort: as is often said, sometimes, in order to change people, you have to change people.

Cultures emerge from thousands of different transactions that occur in organizations every day. Over time, they create a type of hard-wired circuitry that governs how things get done. Even the word 'culture' implies some type of mystical force that floats above the business exerting a magical influence. In reality, it's just a collection of business norms. Changing these norms requires the leader to personally dig into each corner of the business, break the circuitry that has been established and rewire things in a different way. Once severed, it's common for the wiring to reconnect several times. Persistence is critical – you may need to repeat the process, and explain the rationale, multiple times before it sticks. I once heard Jack Welch say that when he set out to break up the bureaucratic culture at General Electric, he had to repeat the same message so many times that he choked on the words.

In my experience, creating a feedback culture is one of the most difficult types of change effort. The multitude of human factors that complicate the effectiveness of feedback get in the way of making feedback a central part of company culture. The variety and intensity of these human factors are often just too much to battle effectively.

However, by eliminating hierarchy and putting the focus on activities and outcomes, something magical happens. People become engaged, defences drop and individuals come to grips more easily with their own shortfalls (thereby avoiding many of the human complications of feedback). I've seen it work in many kinds of organization – from sports franchises to multi-billion-dollar publicly traded companies.

CONCLUSION

"As a manager, you owe candor to your people."[261]

Jack Welch, ex-CEO of General Electric

In today's environment of increasing speed and complexity, it is human performance that makes the difference. In your leadership role, you have a unique opportunity (and responsibility!) to connect, align, inspire and challenge. That opportunity is lost if there is a lack of honest, focused and timely performance feedback. It is a major constraint to individual, team and – ultimately – organizational performance.

It is true that managers don't like difficult conversations. And employees, too, may be recalcitrant, or just pretend to care, or genuinely not 'hear' the message. But it is the leader's job to address all these difficulties, through timely and accurate feedback.

The good news? You are now able to face the environment with a powerful tool that drives performance: FairTalk. It is based on the principles of fairness, focus and credibility. It is a proven way to drive results.

We have given you the facts and science behind human performance and the role of feedback.

Performance is a function of the 3 Cs of performance – competence, characteristics and context. You can use this framework to understand any performance gap in your team. If the issue is competence, you will set expectations for future development. If the issue is characteristics, you will be mindful of what can and can't change. You will focus improvement on what is possible and not ask for what can't be delivered. You will also assess context and modify or temper your feedback based on that. This way, it will always be fair.

Even with great feedback, we've said it before: improving is tough. People are often unaware of their own limitations. Low self-awareness isn't the result of a rampant ego – it's simply the human condition. Your role is to help team members see what they cannot see – through feedback.

You've learned that, even with clear feedback, some team members will not see the point in changing. Others won't believe in their own ability to grow. Your role is to connect feedback to purpose and meaning, and to share an expectation for development. In these cases, feedback is your not-so-secret weapon.

How will you do it? Begin with a proper diagnosis. Defining 'what matters' is the critical departure point for FairTalk. By focusing on the most impactful performance opportunity, you can help employees improve where it matters most. Checking your diagnosis with others will enhance the accuracy of your assessment. It will also temper your own unconscious biases. This makes your feedback fair.

The simple three-part FairTalk Statement will transform your diagnosis into an expectation for change. And it is immensely powerful. It connects people to purpose. Emphasizing the importance of their work reinforces the team member's critical role. It helps to depersonalize feedback, reducing defensiveness and supporting listening. And it forces you, as a leader, to focus feedback on the essentials.

Fairness requires honesty. A FairTalk Statement always includes a clear point of view on how performance compares with expectations. We truly believe in putting performance first.

This powerful statement builds to finally empower your employees to act on their personal growth. By setting an expectation for future development, you engage your employees. The fact that the expectation is future focused increases receptiveness. The fact that it is now a *developmental* expectation or goal ensures growth. Yet it does not fail to make accountability clear.

Once you have delivered the three-part statement, you can pivot the conversation on to coaching. And don't forget to follow up.

There are some traps along the way. We singled out three: skills, emotions and boundaries. You now have the skills and tools to ensure that you don't give baffling, bogus or brutal feedback. Instead of helping, these can harm the person and diminish your credibility.

Your emotions can take over and derail your best attempts. Preparation and practice help you to manage your emotions. And reframing feedback, linking giving feedback to your own core values, can provide you with a compelling reason to act, even when your instincts would have you do otherwise.

Being aware of boundaries, such as culture, gender or hierarchy, will ensure your message docsn't fall flat. You are now equipped with the tips and tools to avoid these traps and ace even the most difficult feedback conversation.

When you consider these factors, your FairTalk message will be relevant, focused, fair, developmental, sincere, sensitive to context, useful and... practically perfect. And you know what? It doesn't need to be perfect. It is more important that it is done.

This final template (TABLE 9) pulls together all the feedback delivery issues that we have discussed in this book. This is your quality control. It enables you to prepare your feedback and consider all the variables, in just a single page.

TABLE 9: FairTalk Statement preparation template

	FEEDBACK CONSIDERATIONS
Why does this issue matter to our results and outcomes? Why is it important to my employee's performance? Is this issue worthy of feedback? Is it the most critical issue? ...	☐ Have I assumed positive intent? ☐ Is it about what and how, not who (i.e. not personal)? ☐ Is it focused? Is it a micro-skill someone could practise? ☐ It is bias free? Did I check this myself or with others?
How is my employee doing? How does their performance align with expectations? (Use examples, facts and balanced opinions.) ...	☐ Have I modified my feedback to take account of context? ☐ Is it usable feedback? ☐ Is it potentially harmful? Have I checked for the 3 Bs (baffling, bogus, brutal)?
What are my expectations for the employee's development, so that performance is improved, going forward? ...	☐ Can I deliver it in a credible manner? ☐ Am I well prepared to control my emotions? ☐ Am I well prepared for the emotional response of the receiver?

Delivering feedback using the FairTalk principles makes the process easier for you, the leader. Importantly, it also makes change easier for the learner. We have given evidence that supports the idea that anyone can change – even people who don't like feedback! When feedback is consistently delivered in the right way, even those sceptical of it can change their attitude to be positive and accepting.[262]

Seeing your people grow and perform is rewarding. Don't stop there. Amplify your impact. Build a FairTalk Culture in your team or organization.

The simple diagnostic in Chapter 13 will identify the cultural levers you need to pull to raise your team to higher performance through feedback. Those may be visible and tangible elements, such as structure and technology, or softer aspects, such as policies and capabilities. You've learned by now that, when it comes to culture, the soft stuff is hard. Your leadership and robust change management are therefore essential to make the hard and soft machinery function.

FairTalk is an overarching approach to improving performance. It goes beyond focusing on the individual. It also helps to create a culture where fair, focused and credible feedback is the language of high performance. As a leader, you build individual skills and capabilities to give and receive feedback. But, at the same time, you pull the organizational levers to build a FairTalk Culture.

We have left our comments on leadership until last, because of its importance. As a leader, you set the tone. Here is some powerful messaging for building a feedback culture in your organization:

- **Know**. Start with the science. Equip your team and organization with the facts about performance feedback. Feedback drives performance when it is fair, focused and delivered by a credible source.
- **Say**. Set the tone. FairTalk is feedback on things that matter, delivered in a way that enables high performance. Say why you are making the issue a priority.

- **Do**. Ask for feedback. Give feedback. Require that feedback be given. Provide practical support to leaders to craft quality feedback. Having made it easy, there must be 'teeth' in the process (consequences for not doing it).
- **Believe**. This is hard work. Stay on message. Don't abandon your culture change initiatives in response to short-term trends or fads, even if you have to go countercultural. With consistency come results. With results comes confidence.

In her book *Act Like a Leader, Think Like a Leader*, Herminia Ibarra reverses the long-held opinion that we need to think and believe certain things before we behave in ways that are consistent with those beliefs. She brings to the fore the idea of 'outsight': behaving like a leader first will lead you to start thinking like one.[263]

So start today. Start giving feedback and demand that others do it in your team and organization, even if you aren't fully convinced that the rewards will outweigh the effort. Behave like a leader.

And, while human performance is complex, there is no shortage of scientific evidence on what increases performance. Feedback is one element. It lends itself perfectly to a structured approach that connects feedback to strategy, to considerations of what and how, to context, and to performance outcomes.

Through feedback, your employees will grow. Your results will grow. Your culture will develop. Your leadership brand will build. Because of your performance, and how you achieve it, you will stand out. Like the feedback you give, you'll have a reputation as fair, focused and credible. Your options will become more numerous, lucrative and varied. Performance from a feedback-rich organization can't easily be replicated. As such, it is a source of advantage for any leader who can deliver it.

A FairTalk leader.

NOTES

1   Feedback to the authors from Lucien Alziari, chief HR officer, CHRO Prudential, August 2018.

2   These findings were first published in Lane, A. M., & Gorbatov, S. (2017). Fair talk: Moving beyond the conversation in search of increased and better feedback. *Performance Improvement*, 56(10), 6–14. doi:10.1002/pfi.21731

3   Feedback to the authors from Jay Zimmerman, talent leader, Aon, August 2018.

4   Bandiera, O., Larcinese, V., & Rasul, I. (2015). Blissful ignorance? A natural experiment on the effect of feedback on students' performance. *Labour Economics*, 34, 13–25. doi:10.1016/j.labeco.2015.02.002

5   Gorbatov, S., & Lane, A. (2018). Is HR missing the point on performance feedback? *MIT Sloan Management Review*, 59(4), 65–71.

6   Moss, S. E., & Sanchez, J. I. (2004). Are your employees avoiding you? Managerial strategies for closing the feedback gap. *Academy of Management Executive*, 18(1), 32–44. doi:10.5465/AME.2004.12691168

7   Moss, S. E., Valenzi, E. R., & Taggart, W. (2003). Are you hiding from your boss? The development of a taxonomy and instrument to assess the feedback management behaviors of good and bad performers. *Journal of Management*, 29(4), 487–510. doi:10.1016/S0149-2063_03_00022-9

8   Anseel, F., Beatty, A. S., Shen, W., Lievens, F., & Sackett, P. R. (2015). How are we doing after 30 years? A meta-analytic review of the antecedents and outcomes of feedback-seeking behavior. *Journal of Management*, 41(1), 318–348. doi:10.1177/0149206313484521

9   Rasheed, A., Khan, S.-U.-R., Rasheed, M. F., & Munir, Y. (2015). The impact of feedback orientation and the effect of satisfaction with feedback on in-role job performance. *Human Resource Development Quarterly*, 26(1), 31–51. doi:10.1002/hrdq.21202

10 Kinicki, A. J., Prussia, G. E., Wu, B. (J.), & McKee-Ryan, F. M. (2004). A covariance structure analysis of employees' response to performance feedback. *Journal of Applied Psychology*, 89(6), 1057–1069. doi:10.1037/0021-9010.89.6.1057

11 Lam, C. F., DeRue, D. S., Karam, E. P., & Hollenbeck, J. R. (2011). The impact of feedback frequency on learning and task performance: Challenging the "more is better" assumption. *Organizational Behavior and Human Decision Processes*, 116(2), 217–228. doi:10.1016/j.obhdp.2011.05.002

12 Casas-Arce, P., Lourenço, S. M., & Martínez-Jerez, F. A. (2017). The performance effect of feedback frequency and detail: Evidence from a field experiment in customer satisfaction. *Journal of Accounting Research*, 55(5), 1051–1088. doi:10.1111/1475-679X.12184

13 Ibid.

14 Lombardo, M. M., & Eichinger, R. W. (2012). *Leadership machine* (10th anniv. ed.). (n.p.): Lominger International, p. 127.

15 Audia, P. G., Locke, E. A., & Smith, K. G. (2000). The paradox of success: An archival and a laboratory study of strategic persistence following radical environmental change. *Academy of Management Journal*, 43(5), 837–853. doi:10.2307/1556413

16 Sharma, R. [@RobinSharma]. (2013, September 20). Negative feedback can make us bitter or better. Retrieved from https://twitter.com/robinsharma/status/381087770761916416.

17 Van-Dijk, D., & Kluger, A. N. (2004). Feedback sign effect on motivation: Is it moderated by regulatory focus? *Applied Psychology*, 53(1), 113–135. doi:10.1111/j.1464-0597.2004.00163.x

18 Ibid.

19 London, M., & Smither, J. W. (2002). Feedback orientation, feedback culture, and the longitudinal performance management process. *Human Resource Management Review*, 12(1), 81–100. doi:10.1016/s1053-4822(01)00043-2

20 Tenney, E. R., Logg, J. M., & Moore, D. A. (2015). (Too) optimistic about optimism: The belief that optimism improves performance. *Journal of Personality and Social Psychology*, 108(3), 377–399. doi:10.1037/pspa0000018

21 Warrenfeltz, R., & Kellett, T. (2015). *Coaching the dark side of personality: High impact strategies to build a winning leadership reputation.* Tulsa, OK: Hogan Assessment Systems, pp. 30–31.

22 Sommer, K. L., & Kulkarni, M. (2012). Does constructive performance feedback improve citizenship intentions and job satisfaction? The roles of perceived opportunities for advancement, respect, and mood. *Human Resource Development Quarterly*, 23(2), 177–201. doi:10.1002/hrdq.21132

23 Kluger, A. N., & DeNisi, A. (1996). The effects of feedback interventions on performance: A historical review, a meta-analysis, and a preliminary feedback intervention theory. *Psychological Bulletin*, 119(2), 254–284. doi:10.1037/0033-2909.119.2.254

24 Godin, S. (2010, February 04). What's expected vs. what's amazing. Retrieved November 5, 2018, from https://seths.blog/2010/02/whats-expected-vs-whats-amazing/

25 Just consider this research finding. In high complexity jobs, correlations between cognitive ability and work performance are in the upper .50s to .60s range. However, even for the lowest complexity jobs, correlations still tend to be substantial – in the .30–.40 range. Source: Kuncel, N. R., Ones, D. S., & Sackett, P. R. (2010). Individual differences as predictors of work, educational, and broad life outcomes. *Personality and Individual Differences*, 49(4), 331–336. doi:10.1016/j.paid.2010.03.042

26 Lasse, C. (2015). What is a competency? *ATD*. Retrieved 20 October 2018 from https://www.td.org/insights/what-is-a-competency

27 McCrae, R. R., & John, O. P. (1992). An introduction to the five-factor model and its applications. *Journal of Personality*, 60(2), 175–215. doi:10.1111/j.1467-6494.1992.tb00970.x

28 Kuncel et al. (2010) set the validities for the Big Five dimensions of personality in the .2–.4 range. This is corroborated by Schmitt (2014), who states that the corrected correlations for personality rarely exceed .25 in predicting individual performance. See Kuncel, Ones, D. S., & Sackett, P. R. (2010). Individual differences as predictors of work, educational, and broad life outcomes. *Personality and Individual Differences*, 49(4), 331–336; Schmitt, N. (2014). Personality and cognitive ability as predictors of effective performance at work. *Annual Review of Organizational Psychology and Organizational Behavior*, 1(1), 45–65. doi:10.1146/annurev-orgpsych-031413-091255

29 According to a robust meta-analytical study, personality has a .48 multiple correlation with leadership. See Judge, T. A., Bono, J. E., Illies, R., & Gerhardt, M. W. (2002). Personality and leadership: A qualitative and quantitative review. *Journey of Applied Psychology*, 87(4), 765–780. doi:10.1037//0021-9010.87.4.765

30 Amazon Jobs. (n.d.). "Leadership principles." Retrieved 20 October 2018 from https://www.amazon.jobs/principles

31 Locke, E. A., & Latham, G. P. (2002). Building a practically useful theory of goal setting and task motivation: A 35-year odyssey. *American Psychologist*, 57(9), 705–717. doi:10.1037/0003-066X.57.9.705

32 We thank Alan Colquitt (author and research scientist, Center for Effective Organizations) for sharing these findings with us.

33 Klug, H. J. P., & Maier, G. W. (2014). Linking goal progress and subjective well-being: A meta-analysis. *Journal of Happiness Studies*, 16(1), 37–65. doi:10.1007/s10902-013-9493-0

34 Lyubomirsky, S., King, L., & Diener, E. (2005). The benefits of frequent positive affect: Does happiness lead to success? *Psychological Bulletin*, 131(6), 803–855. doi:10.1037/0033-2909.131.6.803

35 Amabile, T., & Kramer, S. (2011). *The progress principle: Using small wins to ignite joy, engagement, and creativity at work*. Boston, MA: Harvard Business Press.

36 Parks, L., & Guay, R. P. (2009). Personality, values, and motivation. *Personality and Individual Differences*, 47(7), 675–684. doi:10.1016/j.paid.2009.06.002

37 Huckman, R. S., & Pisano, G. P. (2006). The firm specificity of individual performance: Evidence from cardiac surgery. *Management Science*, 52(4), 473–488. doi:10.1287/mnsc.1050.0464

38 Groysberg, B., Lee, L.-E., & Nanda, A. (2008). Can they take it with them? The portability of star knowledge workers' performance. *Management Science*, 54(7), 1213–1230. doi:10.1287/mnsc.1070.0809

39 If you search for "smell of the place Ghoshal" on YouTube, you will find the video recording of this great speech.

40 Look for this inspirational speech on YouTube by searching for "Chief of Army Lieutenant General David Morrison message about unacceptable behaviour".

41 Meta-analytical evidence suggests that self-efficacy has a .38 correlation with work performance. Stajkovic, A. D., & Luthans, F. (1998). Self-efficacy and work-related performance: A meta-analysis. *Psychological Bulletin*, 124(2), 240–261. doi:10.1037/0033-2909.124.2.240

42 Gottfredson, R. K., & Aguinis, H. (2017). Leadership behaviors and follower performance: Deductive and inductive examination of theoretical rationales and underlying mechanisms. *Journal of Organizational Behavior*, 38(4), 558–591. doi:10.1002/job.2152; Martin, R., Guillaume, Y., Thomas, G., Lee, A., & Epitropaki, O. (2016). Leader–member exchange (LMX) and performance: A meta-analytic review. *Personnel Psychology*, 69(1), 67–121. doi:10.1111/peps.12100

43 Mueller-Hanson, R. A., & Pulakos, E. (2018). *Transforming performance management to drive performance*. New York, NY: Routledge.

44 See Bryant, A. (2011, 12 March). Google's quest to build a better boss. *New York Times*. Retrieved 20 October 2018 http://www.nytimes.com/2011/03/13/business/13hire.html? pagewanted=all&_r=0; Corporate Executive Board. (2004). *Driving employee performance and retention through engagement: A quantitative analysis of the effectiveness of employee engagement strategies*. Washington, DC: Author.

45 Mueller-Hanson, R. A., & Pulakos, E. D. (2018). *Transforming performance management to drive performance: An evidence-based roadmap*. New York, NY: Routledge.

46 Corporate Executive Board. (2012). *Driving breakthrough performance in the new work environment*. Washington, DC: Author.

47   Gibran, K. (1996). *The Prophet*. Hertfordshire: Wordsworth Editions Limited, p. 19.

48   Svenson, O. (1981). Are we all less risky and more skillful than our fellow drivers? *Acta Psychologica*, 47(2), 143–148.

49   Lombardo, M. M., & Eichinger, R. W. (2011). *Leadership machine* (10th anniv. ed.). (n.p.): Lominger International.

50   Beer, J. S., & Hughes, B. L. (2010). Neural systems of social comparison and the 'above-average' effect. *NeuroImage*, 49(3), 2671–2679. doi:10.1016/j. neuroimage.2009.10.075

51   Sutton, C. D., & Woodman, R. W. (1989). Pygmalion goes to work: The effects of supervisor expectations in a retail setting. *Journal of Applied Psychology*, 74(6), 943–950. doi:10.1037/0021-9010.74.6.943. Correlations between adjusted sales and performance appraisal were .50, .37 and .26, *p* < .001 for the three time periods. Correlations between self-expectations and performance appraisal were, respectively, .09, .07 and .15, *non-significant*.

52   Heidemeier, H., & Moser, K. (2009). Self–other agreement in job performance ratings: A meta-analytic test of a process model. *Journal of Applied Psychology*, 94(2), 353–370. doi:10.1037/0021-9010.94.2.353

53   Eurich, T. (2018, 4 January). What self-awareness really is (and how to cultivate it). *Harvard Business Review*. Retrieved 20 October 2018 from https://hbr. org/2018/01/what-self-awareness-really-is-and-how-to-cultivate-it

54   Feedback to the authors from Tomas Chamorro-Premuzic, July 2018.

55   Newman, L. (2014, 30 April). How to give workers better feedback. *Wall Street Journal*. Retrieved 25 July 2017 from https://blogs.wsj.com/experts/2014/04/30/ how-to-give-workers-better-feedback

56   Atwater, L. E., & Yammarino, F. J. (1992). Does self–other agreement on leadership perceptions moderate the validity of leadership and performance predictions? *Personnel Psychology*, 45(1), 141–164. doi:10.1111/j.1744-6570.1992.tb00848.x

57   Feedback to the authors from Lucien Alziari, chief HR officer, CHRO Prudential, August 2018.

58   See, for example, Lucas, R. E., Clark, A. E., Georgellis, Y., & Diener, E. (2003). Reexamining adaptation and the set point model of happiness: Reactions to changes in marital status. *Journal of Personality and Social Psychology*, 84(3), 527–539. doi:10.1037/0022-3514.84.3.527; Fujita, F., & Diener, E. (2005). Life satisfaction set point: Stability and change. *Journal of Personality and Social Psychology*, 88(1), 158–164. doi:10.1037/0022-3514.88.1.158

59   A quote by Victor Hugo. (n.d.). Retrieved November 5, 2018, from https://www. goodreads.com/quotes/369798-being-good-is-easy-what-is-difficult-is-being-just

60   Tabibnia, G., Satpute, A. B., & Lieberman, M. D. (2008). The sunny side of fairness: Preference for fairness activates reward circuitry (and disregarding unfairness activates self-control circuitry). *Psychological Science*, 19(4), 339–347.

61   Bauwens, R., Audenaert, M., Huisman, J., & Decramer, A. (2017). Performance management fairness and burnout: Implications for organizational citizenship behaviors. *Studies in Higher Education*. doi:10.1080/03075079.2017.1389878

62   Sparr, J. L., & Sonnentag, S. (2008). Fairness perceptions of supervisor feedback, LMX, and employee well-being at work. *European Journal of Work and Organizational Psychology*, 17(2), 198–225. doi:10.1080/13594320701743590

63   Ibid.

64 Van Dierendonck, D., & Jacobs, G. (2012). Survivors and victims, a meta analytical review of fairness and organizational commitment after downsizing. *British Journal of Management*, 23(1), 96–109.

65 See Gorbatov, S., & Lane, A, (2018). Is HR missing the point on performance feedback? *MIT Sloan Management Review*. Retrieved 22 October 2018 from https://sloanreview.mit.edu/article/is-hr-missing-the-point-on-performance-feedback; Mueller-Hanson, R. A., & Pulakos, E. D. (2018). Transforming performance management to drive performance: An evidence-based roadmap. New York, NY: Routledge.

66 Feedback to the authors from Elaine Pulakos, president, PDRI, August 2018.

67 Chory, R. M., & Kingsley Westerman, C. Y. (2009). Feedback and fairness: The relationship between negative performance feedback and organizational justice. *Western Journal of Communication*, 73(2), 157–181, p. 171. doi:10.1080/10570310902856055

68 Kluger, A. N., & DeNisi, A. (1996). The effects of feedback interventions on performance: A historical review, a meta-analysis, and a preliminary feedback intervention theory. *Psychological Bulletin*, 119(2), 254–284. doi:10.1037/0033-2909.119.2.254

69 Falk, A., Fehr, E., & Fischbacher, U. (2008). Testing theories of fairness: Intentions matter. *Games and Economic Behavior*, 62(1), 287–303. doi:10.1016/j.geb.2007.06.001

70 Chory, R. M., & Kingsley Westerman, C. Y. (2009). Feedback and fairness: The relationship between negative performance feedback and organizational justice. *Western Journal of Communication*, 73(2), 157–181, p. 171. doi:10.1080/10570310902856055

71 Feedback to the authors from Lucien Alziari, chief HR officer, CHRO Prudential, August 2018.

72 Feedback to the authors from Rob Kaiser, president, Kaiser Leadership Solutions, October 2018.

73 Busy bosses often seem unfair. (2018). *Harvard Business Review*, 96(5), 28.

74 Jawahar, I. M. (2010). The mediating role of appraisal feedback reactions on the relationship between rater feedback-related behaviors and ratee performance. *Group & Organization Management*, 35(4), 494–526. doi:10.1177/1059601110378294

75 Harrison, S. H., & Dossinger, K. (2017). Pliable guidance: A multilevel model of curiosity, feedback seeking, and feedback giving in creative work. *Academy of Management Journal*, 60(6), 2051–2072. doi:10.5465/amj.2015.0247

76 Goodman, J. S., Wood, R. E., & Chen, Z. (2011). Feedback specificity, information processing, and transfer of training. *Organizational Behavior and Human Decision Processes*, 115(2), 253–267. doi:10.1016/j.obhdp.2011.01.001

77 Anseel, F., Lievens, F., & Schollaert, E. (2009). Reflection as a strategy to enhance task performance after feedback. *Organizational Behavior and Human Decision Processes*, 110(1), 23–35. doi:10.1016/j.obhdp.2009.05.003

78 Kinicki, A. J., Prussia, G. E., Wu, B., & McKee-Ryan, F. M. (2004). A covariance structure analysis of employees' response to performance feedback. *Journal of Applied Psychology*, 89(6), 1057–1069.

79 Lechermeier, J., & Fassnacht, M. (2018). How do performance feedback characteristics influence recipients' reactions? A state-of-the-art review on feedback source, timing, and valence effects. *Management Review Quarterly*, 68(2), 145–193. doi:10.1007/s11301-018-0136-8

80 Edelman. (2018). *2018 Edelman trust barometer: Global report.*
    Retrieved 20 October 2018 from https://www.edelman.com/sites/g/files/aatuss191/
    files/2018-10/2018_Edelman_Trust_Barometer_Global_Report_FEB.pdf

81 McCroskey, J., & Teven, J. (1999). Goodwill: A reexamination of the
    construct and its measurement. *Communication Monographs, 66*(1), 90–103.
    doi:10.1080/03637759909376464

82 Adapted from McCroskey, J., & Teven, J. (1999). Goodwill: A reexamination of
    the construct and its measurement. *Communication Monographs, 66*(1), 90–103.
    doi:10.1080/03637759909376464

83 Lu, K.-M., Pan, S.-Y., & Cheng, J.-W. (2011). Examination of a perceived cost model
    of employees' negative feedback-seeking behavior. *Journal of Psychology, 145*(6),
    573–594. doi:10.1080/00223980.2011.613873

84 Brooks, A. W., Gino, F., & Schweitzer, M. E. (2015). Smart people ask for (my)
    advice: Seeking advice boosts perceptions of competence. *Management Science,
    61*(6), 1421–1435. doi:10.1287/mnsc.2014.2054

85 Ashford, S. J., De Stobbeleir, K., & Nujella, M. (2016). To seek or not to seek: Is
    that the only question? Recent developments in feedback-seeking literature. *Annual
    Review of Organizational Psychology and Organizational Behavior, 3*(1), 213–239.
    doi:10.1146/annurev-orgpsych-041015-062314

86 Chamorro-Premuzic, T. (2017). *The talent delusion: Why data, not intuition, is the
    key to unlocking human potential.* London, UK: Hachette, p. 224.

87 Arthur, M. B., Khapova, S. N., & Richardson, J. (2016). *An intelligent career: Taking
    ownership of your work and your life.* New York, NY: Oxford University Press.

88 Atlee, T. (2003). Crisis Fatigue and the Co-Creation of Positive Possibilities. Retrieved
    November 5, 2018, from https://www.co-intelligence.org/crisis_fatigue.html

89 Drucker, P. F. (1959). *Landmarks of tomorrow.* Harper, NYC, 1959, p. 120.

90 Ocean Tomo. (2015, 5 March). Annual study of intangible asset
    market value. Retrieved 20 October 2018 from http://www.oceantomo.
    com/2015/03/04/2015-intangible-asset-market-value-study

91 Bort, J. (2015). Marissa Mayer defends her famous ban on remote work:
    'I hope that's not my legacy'. *Business Insider.* Retrieved 20 October 2018
    https://www.businessinsider.com/mayer-still-defends-remote-work-ban-2015-11

92 Simons, J. (2017). IBM, a pioneer of remote work, calls workers back to the office.
    Wall Street Journal. Retrieved 20 October 2018 from https://www.wsj.com/articles/
    ibm-a-pioneer-of-remote-work-calls-workers-back-to-the-office-1495108802

93 Lublin, J. (2017, 1 November). They're talking behind my
    back: Remote workers feel unsupported. *Wall Street Journal.*
    Retrieved 20 October 2018 from https://www.wsj.com/articles/
    theyre-talking-behind-my-back-remote-workers-feel-unsupported-1509541381

94 Sargut, G., & McGrath, R. G. (2011). Learning to live with complexity. *Harvard
    Business Review, 89*(9), 68–76, 136.

95 Paradoxically, the complex technology has made our jobs simpler. Some scholars
    argue that the impact of the increased complexity in the workplace is grossly
    exaggerated. Chamorro-Premuzic, T. (2017). *The talent delusion: Why data, not
    intuition, is the key to unlocking human potential.* London, UK: Hachette.

96 Arthur, M. B., Khapova, S. N., & Richardson, J. (2016). *An intelligent career: Taking
    ownership of your work and your life.* New York, NY: Oxford University Press.

97 Greenhaus, J. H., & Kossek, E. E. (2014). The contemporary career: A work–home perspective. *Annual Review of Organizational Psychology and Organizational Behavior*, 1(1), 361–388. doi:10.1146/annurev-orgpsych-031413-091324

98 Hamori, M., Koyuncu, B., Cao, J., & Graf, T. (2015). What high-potential young managers want. *MIT Sloan Management Review*, 57(1), 61–68, p. 63.

99 Craig, E., Kimberly, J., & Cheese, P. (2009). How to keep your best executives. *Wall Street Journal*. Retrieved 20 October 2018 from https://www.wsj.com/articles/SB10001424052970203946904574302011865406286

100 Weber, Lauren. (2017, 2 February). The end of employees. *Wall Street Journal*. Retrieved 5 July 2017 from https://www.wsj.com/articles/the-end-of-employees-1486050443

101 Avent, R. (2018). Crafting a Life. *The Economist*. Retrieved 20 October 2018 from https://www.1843magazine.com/features/crafting-a-life

102 Aarons-Mele, M. (2014). The dangerous rise of 'entrepreneurship porn'. Retrieved 20 October 2018 from https://hbr.org/2014/01/the-dangerous-rise-of-entrepreneurship-porn

103 Mann, A., & Harter, J. (2016, 7 January). The worldwide employee engagement crisis. *Gallup*. Retrieved 20 October 2018 from http://news.gallup.com/businessjournal/188033/worldwide-employee-engagement-crisis.aspx

104 Edelman. (2018). *2018 Edelman trust barometer: Global report*. Retrieved 20 October 2018 from http://cms.edelman.com/sites/default/files/2018-02/2018_Edelman_Trust_Barometer_Global_Report_FEB.pdf

105 See the introduction to Part One for a reminder of the categories.

106 Hamori, M., Koyuncu, B., Cao, J., & Graf, T. (2015). What high-potential young managers want. MIT Sloan Management Review, 57(1), 61–68.

107 Allen, D. (2004). Ready for Anything: 52 Productivity Principles for Getting Things Done. Penguin, p. 34.

108 Chamorro-Premuzic, T. (2017). *The talent delusion: Why data, not intuition, is the key to unlocking human potential*. London, UK: Hachette.

109 Howell, J. L., & Ratliff, K. A. (2017). Not your average bigot: The better-than-average effect and defensive responding to implicit association test feedback. *British Journal of Social Psychology*, 56(1), 125–145. doi:10.1111/bjso.12168

110 Kahneman, D. (2011). *Thinking, fast and slow*. New York, NY: Farrar, Straus and Giroux, p. 85.

111 Viswesvaran, C., Ones, D. S., & Schmidt, F. L. (1996). Comparative analysis of the reliability of job performance ratings. *Journal of Applied Psychology*, 81(5), 557–574. doi:10.1037/0021-9010.81.5.557

112 Roch, S. G., McNall, L. A., & Caputo, P. M. (2011). Self-judgments of accuracy as indicators of performance evaluation quality: Should we believe them? *Journal of Business and Psychology*, 26(1), 41–55. doi:10.1007/s10869-010-9173-6

113 Bohnet, I., Van Geen, A., & Bazerman, M. (2015). When performance trumps gender bias: Joint vs. separate evaluation. *Management Science*, 62(5), 1225–1234.

114 Willemsen, M. C., & Keren, G. (2004). The role of negative features in joint and separate evaluation. *Journal of Behavioral Decision Making*, 17(4), 313–329.

115 Kaiser, R. (Ed.). (2005). *Filling the leadership pipeline*. NJ: Center for Creative Leadership; Kaplan, B., & Kaiser, R. (2006). *The versatile leader*. San Francisco, CA: John Wiley & Sons; Kaiser, R. (2009). *The perils of accentuating the positive*. Tulsa, OK: Hogan Press.

116 Feedback to the authors from Jay Zimmerman, talent leader, Aon, August 2018.

117 Northcraft, G. B., Schmidt, A. M., & Ashford, S. J. (2011). Feedback and the rationing of time and effort among competing tasks. *Journal of Applied Psychology*, 96(5), 1076–1086. doi:10.1037/a0023221

118 We first introduced the model in Lane, A. M., & Gorbatov, S. (2017). Fair talk: Moving beyond the conversation in search of increased and better feedback. *Performance Improvement*, 56(10), 6–14. doi:10.1002/pfi.21731

119 Langer, E. J., Blank, A., & Chanowitz, B. (1978). The mindlessness of ostensibly thoughtful action: The role of 'placebic' information in interpersonal interaction. *Journal of Personality and Social Psychology*, 36(6), 635–642. doi:10.1037/0022-3514.36.6.635

120 Feedback to the authors from Kate Sweetman, founding principal, SweetmanCragun Group, July 2018.

121 Feedback to the authors from Professor Konstantin Korotov, European School of Management and Technology, May 2018.

122 Pink, D. H. (2010). *Drive: The surprising truth about what motivates us.* Edinburgh, UK: Canongate Books. See also Chapter 4 for the key tenets of the goal-setting theory.

123 Hogan, R., & Kaiser, R. B. (2005). What we know about leadership. *Review of General Psychology*, 9(2), 169–180. doi:10.1037/1089-2680.9.2.169

124 Lam, C. F., DeRue, D. S., Karam, E. P., & Hollenbeck, J. R. (2011). The impact of feedback frequency on learning and task performance: Challenging the 'more is better' assumption. *Organizational Behavior and Human Decision Processes*, 116(2), 217–228. doi:10.1016/j.obhdp.2011.05.002

125 Feedback to the authors from Jay Zimmerman, talent leader, Aon, August 2018.

126 Baumeister, R. F., Dale, K., & Sommer, K. L. (1998). Freudian defense mechanisms and empirical findings in modern social psychology: Reaction formation, projection, displacement, undoing, isolation, sublimation, and denial. *Journal of Personality*, 66(6), 1081–1124. doi:10.1111/1467-6494.00043

127 Feedback to the authors from Lucien Alziari, chief HR officer, CHRO Prudential, August 2018.

128 Kluger, A. N., & DeNisi, A. (1996). The effects of feedback interventions on performance: A historical review, a meta-analysis, and a preliminary feedback intervention theory. *Psychological Bulletin*, 119(2), 254–284. doi:10.1037/0033-2909.119.2.254

129 Schmeichel, B. J., Caskey, R., & Hicks, J. A. (2015). Rational versus experiential processing of negative feedback reduces defensiveness but induces ego depletion. *Self and Identity*, 14(1), 75–89. doi:10.1080/15298868.2014.952772

130 Goldsmith, M. (n.d.). Try feedforward instead of feedback. Retrieved 20 October 2018 from http://www.marshallgoldsmithfeedforward.com/html/Articles.htm

131 VandeWalle, D., Cron, W. L., & Slocum, J. W. (2001). The role of goal orientation following performance feedback. *Journal of Applied Psychology*, 86(4), 629–640. doi:10.1037/0021-9010.86.4.629

132 Feedback to the authors from Jeff Anderson, president and CEO, Lake Forest Graduate School of Management, September 2018.

133 Boswell, W. R., & Boudreau, J. W. (2002). Separating the developmental and evaluative performance appraisal uses. *Journal of Business and Psychology*, 16(3), 391–412. doi:10.1023/A:1012872907525

134 Rasheed, A., Khan, S.-U.-R., Rasheed, M. F., & Munir, Y. (2015). The impact of feedback orientation and the effect of satisfaction with feedback on in-role job performance. *Human Resource Development Quarterly*, 26(1), 31–51. doi:10.1002/hrdq.21202

135 Zeigarnik, B. (1938). On finished and unfinished tasks. In W. D. Ellis (Ed.), *A source book of Gestalt psychology* (pp. 300–314). London, UK: Kegal Paul, Trench, Trubner & Co.

136 Feedback to the authors from Rob Sheppard, vice president, BTS, April 2018.

137 Feedback to the authors from Jay Zimmerman, talent leader, Aon, August 2018.

138 A quote by T.S. Eliot. (n.d.). Retrieved November 5, 2018, from https://www.goodreads.com/quotes/33904-most-of-the-evil-in-this-world-is-done-by

139 Kluger, A. N., & DeNisi, A. (1996). The effects of feedback interventions on performance: A historical review, a meta-analysis, and a preliminary feedback intervention theory. *Psychological Bulletin*, 119(2), 254–284. doi:10.1037/0033-2909.119.2.254

140 Ibid.

141 Feedback to the authors from Linda Rodman, president, Rodman Resources LLC, August 2018.

142 Ackerman, P. L. (2017). Adult intelligence: The construct and the criterion problem. *Perspectives on Psychological Science*, 12(6), 987–998. doi:10.1177/1745691617703437

143 Nicky, D., & Pepermans, R. (2012). How to identify leadership potential: Development and testing of a consensus model. *Human Resource Management*, 51(3), 361–385.

144 Lombardo, M. M., & Eichinger, R. W. (2011). *Leadership machine* (10th anniv. ed.). (n.p.): Lominger International.

145 While we include this example to make the point that not everyone needs every competency and that not all competencies help performance, there may be occasions when an employee needs to 'lighten up' or laugh at themselves. If this is the case, give feedback.

146 Pritchard, R. D., Youngcourt, S. S., Philo, J. R., McMonagle, D., & David, J. H. (2007). The use of priority information in performance feedback. *Human Performance*, 20(1), 61–83. doi:10.1080/08959280709336929

147 Sims, H. P., Gioia, D. A., & Longenecker, C. O. (1987). Behind the mask: The politics of employee appraisal. *Academy of Management Executive*, 1(3), 183–193. doi:10.5465/AME.1987.4275731

148 Bear, J. B., Cushenbery, L., London, M., & Sherman, G. D. (2017). Performance feedback, power retention, and the gender gap in leadership. *Leadership Quarterly*, 28(6), 721–740. doi:10.1016/j.leaqua.2017.02.003

149 Kollée, J. A. J. M., Giessner, S. R., & Van Knippenberg, D. (2013). Leader evaluations after performance feedback: The role of follower mood. *Leadership Quarterly*, 24(1), 203–214. doi:10.1016/j.leaqua.2012.10.007

150 There are several versions of this anecdote, which makes this an amusing story rather than a historical fact.

151 Raver, J. L., Jensen, J. M., Lee, J., & O'Reilly, J. (2012). Destructive criticism revisited: Appraisals, task outcomes, and the moderating role of competitiveness. *Applied Psychology*, 61(2), 177–203. doi:10.1111/j.1464-0597.2011.00462.x

152 Newcomer, E. (2017, 28 February). In video, Uber CEO argues with driver over falling fares. *Bloomberg Technology*. Retrieved 20 October 2018 from https://www.bloomberg.com/news/articles/2017-02-28/in-video-uber-ceo-argues-with-driver-over-falling-fares

153 Newcomer, E., & Stone, B. (2018, 18 January). The fall of Travis Kalanick was a lot weirder and darker than you thought. *Bloomberg Businessweek*. Retrieved 20 October 2018 from https://www.bloomberg.com/news/features/2018-01-18/the-fall-of-travis-kalanick-was-a-lot-weirder-and-darker-than-you-thought

154 Goulston, M. (2013, 11 March). How to give a meaningful apology. *Harvard Business Review*. Retrieved 20 October 2018 from https://hbr.org/2013/03/how-to-give-a-meaningful-apolo

155 Twenge, J. M., Konrath, S. , Foster, J. D., Keith Campbell, W. and Bushman, B. J. (2008), Egos Inflating Over Time: A Cross Temporal Meta Analysis of the Narcissistic Personality Inventory. *Journal of Personality*, 76: 875-902. doi:10.1111/j.1467-6494.2008.00507.x

156 Feedback to the authors from Marc Effron, president, Talent Strategy Group, September 2018.

157 Feedback to the authors from Lucien Alziari, chief HR officer, CHRO Prudential, August 2018.

158 Hogan, R., & Kaiser, R. B. (2005). What we know about leadership. *Review of General Psychology*, 9(2), 169–180. doi:10.1037/1089-2680.9.2.169

159 Feedback to the authors from Linda Rodman, president, Rodman Resources LLC, September 2018.

160 Hoffman, M. A., Hill, C. E., Holmes, S. E., & Freitas, G. F. (2005). Supervisor perspective on the process and outcome of giving easy, difficult, or no feedback to supervisees. *Journal of Counseling Psychology*, 52(1), 3–13.

161 Kohlrieser, G., Goldsworthy, S., & Coombe, D. (2012). Care to Dare: Unleashing Astonishing Potential Through Secure Base Leadership. Retrieved November 5, 2018, from https://www.google.es/search?tbo=p&tbm=bks&q=isbn:1118361288

162 Dahling, J. J., Chau, S. L., & O'Malley, A. (2012). Correlates and consequences of feedback orientation in organizations. *Journal of Management*, 38(2), 531–546. doi:10.1177/0149206310375467

163 Kashdan, T. B., DeWall, C. N., Pond, R. S., Silvia, P. J., Lambert, N. M., Fincham, F. D. ... Keller, P. S. (2013). Curiosity protects against interpersonal aggression: Cross-sectional, daily process, and behavioral evidence. *Journal of Personality*, 81(1), 87–102. doi:10.1111/j.1467-6494.2012.00783.x

164 Rasheed, A., Khan, S.-U.-R., Rasheed, M. F., & Munir, Y. (2015). The impact of feedback orientation and the effect of satisfaction with feedback on in-role job performance. *Human Resource Development Quarterly*, 26(1), 31–51. doi:10.1002/hrdq.21202

165 In psychology this is termed 'ambivalent', although not in the common use of that term. It is not ambivalent in the sense that it is mixed or indecisive; rather, it refers to the coexistence of two seemingly opposite (positive and negative) feelings. See Harrison, S. H., & Dossinger, K. (2017). Pliable guidance: A multilevel model of curiosity, feedback seeking, and feedback giving in creative work. *Academy of Management Journal*, 60(6), 2051–2072. doi:10.5465/amj.2015.0247

166 Feedback to the authors from Lucien Alziari, chief HR officer, CHRO Prudential, August 2018.

167 Goleman, D., & Boyatzis, R. (2008). Social intelligence and the biology of leadership. *Harvard Business Review*, 86(9), 74–81, pp. 76–77.

168 Motro, D., & Ellis, A. P. J. (2017). Boys, don't cry: Gender and reactions to negative performance feedback. *Journal of Applied Psychology*, 102(2), 227–235, p. 231. doi:10.1037/apl0000175

169 Williams, A. (2014, May 29). Exclusive interview: Maya Angelou from earlier this month. *The Washington Times*. Retrieved November 5, 2018, from https://www.washingtontimes.com/news/2014/may/29/exclusive-interview-maya-angelou-earlier-month/

170 We allude to Thomas L. Friedman's bestselling book *The World Is Flat: A Brief History of the Twenty-First Century* (London, UK: Penguin, 2006), where the author makes a case for rapidly increasing the pace of globalization, leveling the playing field for competition, and removing political, social, technological and organizational boundaries.

171 Miller, D. L., & Karakowsky, L. (2005). Gender influences as an impediment to knowledge sharing: When men and women fail to seek peer feedback. *Journal of Psychology*, 139(2), 101–118. doi:10.3200/JRLP.139.2.101-118

172 Berlin, N., & Dargnies, M.-P. (2016). Gender differences in reactions to feedback and willingness to compete. *Journal of Economic Behavior & Organization*, 130, 320–336. doi:10.1016/j.jebo.2016.08.002

173 Wozniak, D., Harbaugh, W. T., & Mayr, U. (2014). The menstrual cycle and performance feedback alter gender differences in competitive choices. *Journal of Labor Economics*, 32(1), 161–198. doi:10.1086/673324

174 Ibid.

175 Berlin, N., & Dargnies, M.-P. (2016). Gender differences in reactions to feedback and willingness to compete. *Journal of Economic Behavior & Organization*, 130, 320–336. doi:10.1016/j.jebo.2016.08.002

176 Costanza, D. P., Badger, J. M., Fraser, R. L., Severt, J. B., & Gade, P. A. (2012). Generational differences in work-related attitudes: A meta-analysis. *Journal of Business and Psychology*, 27(4), 375–394. doi:10.1007/s10869-012-9259-4

177 Costanza, D. P., & Finkelstein, L. M. (2015). Generationally based differences in the workplace: Is there a there there? *Industrial and Organizational Psychology*, 8(3), 308–323. doi:10.1017/iop.2015.15

178 Meyer, E. (2014). *The culture map: Breaking through the invisible boundaries of global business*. New York, NY: PublicAffairs.

179 Meyer, E. (2016). How to give and receive feedback across cultures. *Fast Company*. Retrieved 20 October 2018 from https://www.fastcompany.com/3056385/how-to-give-and-receive-feedback-across-cultures

180 Barner-Rasmussen, W. (2003). Determinants of the feedback-seeking behaviour of subsidiary top managers in multinational corporations. *International Business Review*, 12(1), 41–60. doi:10.1016/S0969-5931(02)00087-2

181 Learn about these cultural dimensions, compare different countries with each other and much more at https://www.hofstede-insights.com.

182 We borrowed the idea of linking managerial practices to cultural dimensions and the general format for this table from Aguinis, H., Joo, H., & Gottfredson, R. (2012). Performance management universals: Think globally and act locally. *Business Horizons*, 55(4), 385–392. doi:10.1016/j.bushor.2012.03.004

183 Song, H., Tucker, A. L., Murrell, K. L., & Vinson, D. R. (2017). Closing the productivity gap: Improving worker productivity through public relative performance feedback and validation of best practices. *Management Science*, 64(6), 2628–2649. doi:10.1287/mnsc.2017.2745

184 Lin, T. W. (2006). Lessons from China. *Strategic Finance*, 88(4), 48–55.

185 Haier Group. (2015, 20 April). Haier Group's CEO becomes first recipient of major global CEO award for innovative talent management practices. Retrieved 20 October 2018 from https://www.prnewswire.com/news-releases/haier-groups-ceo-becomes-first-recipient-of-major-global-ceo-award-for-innovative-talent-management-practices-300068474.html

186 Lam, L. W., Peng, K. Z., Wong, C.-S., & Lau, D. C. (2017). Is more feedback seeking always better? Leader–member exchange moderates the relationship between feedback-seeking behavior and performance. *Journal of Management*, 43(7), 2195–2217. doi:10.1177/0149206315581661

187 Tannenbaum, S. I., & Cerasoli, C. P. (2013). Do team and individual debriefs enhance performance? A meta-analysis. *Human Factors*, 55(1), 231–245. doi:10.1177/0018720812448394

188 Feedback to the authors from Jeff Anderson, president and CEO, Lake Forest Graduate School of Management, September 2018.

189 Gino, F. (2018). *Rebel talent: Why it pays to break the rules at work and in life.* London, UK: Pan Macmillan.

190 Two insightful books on the topic of unproductive and destructive managerial behaviors are Pfeffer, J. (2015). *Leadership BS: Fixing workplaces and careers one truth at a time.* New York, NY: Harper Business; Culbert, S. A. (2017). *Good people, bad managers.* New York, NY: Oxford University Press.

191 Conway, J. M., & Huffcutt, A. I. (1997). Psychometric properties of multisource performance ratings: A meta-analysis of subordinate, supervisor, peer, and self-ratings. *Human Performance*, 10(4), 331–360. Self–peer correlation was .19 and peer–boss correlation was .34.

192 Kofman, F. (2015). How to escalate disagreements cleanly: A coaching conversation. Retrieved 20 October 2018 from https://www.huffingtonpost.com/fred-kofman/how-to-escalate-disagreem_b_8193382.html?guccounter=1

193 Van der Rijt, J., Van de Wiel, M. W. J., Van den Bossche, P., Segers, M. S. R., & Gijselaers, W. H. (2012). Contextual antecedents of informal feedback in the workplace. *Human Resource Development Quarterly*, 23(2), 233–257. doi:10.0.3.234/hrdq.21129

194 Quoted in Dawkins, R. (Ed.). (2009). *The Oxford book of modern science writing.* Oxford, UK: Oxford University Press, p. 18.

195 Arvey, R. D., Rotundo, M., Johnson, W., Zhang, Z., & McGue, M. (2006). The determinants of leadership role occupancy: Genetic and personality factors. *Leadership Quarterly*, 17(1), 1–20. doi:10.1016/j.leaqua.2005.10.009

196 Arvey, R. D., Zhang, Z., Avolio, B. J., & Krueger, R. F. (2007). Developmental and genetic determinants of leadership role occupancy among women. *Journal of Applied Psychology*, 92(3), 693–706. doi:10.1037/0021-9010.92.3.693

197 Sagi, Y., Tavor, I., Hofstetter, S., Tzur-Moryosef, S., Blumenfeld-Katzir, T., & Assaf, Y. (2012). Learning in the fast lane: New insights into neuroplasticity. *Neuron* 73(6), 1195–1203. doi:10.1016/j.neuron.2012.01.025

198 Dweck, C. S. (2008). Can personality be changed? The role of beliefs in personality and change. *Current Directions in Psychological Science*, 17(6), 391–394. doi:10.1111/j.1467-8721.2008.00612.x

199 Dweck, C. S. (2017). The journey to children's mindsets: And beyond. *Child Development Perspectives*, 11, 139–144. doi:10.1111/cdep.12225

200 Dweck, C. S. (2008). Can personality be changed? The role of beliefs in personality and change. *Current Directions in Psychological Science*, 17(6), 391–394. doi:10.1111/j.1467-8721.2008.00612.x

201 Moser, J. S., Schroder, H. S., Heeter, C., Moran, T. P., & Lee, Y. H. (2011). Mind your errors: Evidence for a neural mechanism linking growth mind-set to adaptive posterror adjustments. *Psychological Science*, 22(12), 1484–1489. doi:10.1177/0956797611419520

202 Job, V., Walton, G. M., Bernecker, K., & Dweck, C. S. (2015). Implicit theories about willpower predict self-regulation and grades in everyday life. *Journal of Personality and Social Psychology*, 108(4), 637–647. doi:10.1037/pspp0000014

203 Dweck, C. S. (2006). *Mindset: The new psychology of success*. New York, NY: Random House.

204 Duhigg, C. (2012). *The power of habit: Why we do what we do, and how to change*. London, UK: Random House.

205 Ibid.

206 Tobias, R. (2009). Changing behavior by memory aids: A social psychological model of prospective memory and habit development tested with dynamic field data. *Psychological Review*, 116(2), 408–438. doi:10.1037/a0015512

207 Colvin, G. (2011). *Talent is overrated: What really separates world-class performers from everybody else*. London, UK: Nicholas Brealey.

208 Goldsmith, M., & Reiter, M. (2015). *Triggers: Creating behavior that lasts – Becoming the person you want to be*. New York, NY: Crown Business.

209 Duhigg, C. (2012). *The power of habit: Why we do what we do, and how to change*. London, UK: Random House.

210 Witherspoon, R. (2014). Double-loop coaching for leadership development. *Journal of Applied Behavioral Science*, 50(3), 261–283. doi:10.1177/0021886313510032

211 Gregersen, H. (2017, March–April). Bursting the CEO bubble: Why executives should talk less and ask more questions. *Harvard Business Review*, 76–83.

212 Brickman, P., Coates, D., & Janoff-Bulman, R. (1978). Lottery winners and accident victims: Is happiness relative? *Journal of Personality and Social Psychology*, 36(8), 917–927. doi:10.1037/0022-3514.36.8.917

213 See research by Dan Ariely from Duke University. Through a series of experiments, he conclusively proves that people are motivated by seeing the progress and being acknowledged for making it.

214 Mellon, L. (2011). *Inside the leader's mind*. Harlow, UK: Prentice Hall; Mellon, L., & Carter, S. (2013). *The strategy of execution*. New York, NY: McGraw-Hill Education.

215 See, for example, James, O. (2013). *Office politics*. London, UK: Vermilion; Babiak, P., & Hare, R. D. (2006). *Snakes in suits*. New York, NY: HarperCollins.

216 Feedback to the authors from Marc Effron, president, Talent Strategy Group, September 2018.

217 Norcross, J. C., & Vangarelli, D. J. (1988). The resolution solution: Longitudinal examination of New Year's change attempts. *Journal of Substance Abuse*, 1(2), 127–134. doi:10.1016/S0899-3289(88)80016-6

218 Hartenian, L. S., Koppes, L. L., & Hartman, E. A. (2002). Performance feedback in a virtual team setting. *Journal of Behavioral and Applied Management*, 4(1), 19–30.

219 Chawla, N., Gabriel, A. S., Dahling, J. J., & Patel, K. (2016). Feedback dynamics are critical to improving performance management systems. *Industrial and Organizational Psychology*, 9(2), 260–266. doi:10.1017/iop.2016.8

220 Van der Rijt, J., Van de Wiel, M. W. J., Van den Bossche, P., Segers, M. S. R., & Gijselaers, W. H. (2012). Contextual antecedents of informal feedback in the workplace. *Human Resource Development Quarterly*, 23(2), 233–257. doi:10.0.3.234/hrdq.21129

221 Whitaker, B. G., Dahling, J. J., & Levy, P. (2007). The development of a feedback environment and role clarity model of job performance. *Journal of Management*, 33(4), 570–591. doi:10.1177/0149206306297581

222 Anseel, F., Beatty, A. S., Shen, W., Lievens, F., & Sackett, P. R. (2015). How are we doing after 30 years? A meta-analytic review of the antecedents and outcomes of feedback-seeking behavior. *Journal of Management,* 41(1), 318–348. doi:10.1177/0149206313484521

223 Gartner. (2018). The real impact of removing performance ratings on employee performance. Retrieved 20 October 2018 from https://www.gartner.com/smarterwithgartner/corporate-hr-removing-performance-ratings-is-unlikely-to-improve-performance/

224 Feedback to the authors from Liz Mellon, chair of the editorial board for *Dialogue Journal,* Duke Corporate Education, July 2018.

225 Tiger, L. (1970). Dominance in human societies. *Annual Review of Ecology and Systematics*, 1(1), 287–306.

226 Stein, S. (2009, 24 May). Larry Summers falls asleep during credit card industry meeting. *HuffPost*. Retrieved 20 October 2018 from https://www.huffingtonpost.com/2009/04/23/larry-summers-falls-aslee_n_190659.html

227 Buckingham, L., & Kane, F. (2014, 22 August). From the archive, 22 August 1992: Gerald Ratner's 'crap' comment haunts jewellery chain. *The Guardian*. Retrieved 20 October 2018 https://www.theguardian.com/business/2014/aug/22/gerald-ratner-jewellery-total-crap-1992-archive

228 Wilbur, H. (2015, 8 October). Ex-Lululemon CEO apologizes for fat-shaming remarks from 2 years ago. *Mashable*. Retrieved 20 October 2018 from https://mashable.com/2015/10/08/lululemon-ceo-apologizes/?europe=true#ASWS.QP38sqA

229 Labich, K. (1994, 2 May). Is Herb Kelleher America's best CEO? Behind his clowning is a people-wise manager who wins where others can't. *CNN Money*. Retrieved 20 October 2018 https://money.cnn.com/magazines/fortune/fortune_archive/1994/05/02/79246/index.htm

230 Feedback to the authors from Kate Sweetman, founding principal, SweetmanCragun Group, July 2018.

231 Bregman, P. (2009, 25 June). A good way to change a corporate culture. *Harvard Business Review*. Retrieved 20 October 2018 from https://hbr.org/2009/06/the-best-way-to-change-a-corpo

232 Feedback to the authors from Jeff Anderson, president and CEO, Lake Forest Graduate School of Management, August 2018.

233 Pritchard, R. D., Youngcourt, S. S., Philo, J. R., McMonagle, D., & David, J. H. (2007). The use of priority information in performance feedback. *Human Performance,* 20(1), 61–83. doi:10.1080/08959280709336929

234 Rosen, C. C., Levy, P. E., & Hall, R. J. (2006). Placing perceptions of politics in the context of the feedback environment, employee attitudes, and job performance. *Journal of Applied Psychology,* 91(1), 211–220. doi:10.1037/0021-9010.91.1.211

235 We modified these items from the utility and accountability sections of the Feedback Orientation Scale developed by Linderbaum, B. A., & Levy, P. E. (2010). The development and validation of the feedback orientation scale (FOS). *Journal of Management,* 36(6), 1372–1405. doi:10.1177/0149206310373145

236 Macneish, J., & Richardson, T. (1994). *The Choice: Either change the system or polish the fruit,* Don't Press, Australia, p. 22.

237 Feedback to the authors from Alan Colquitt, author and research scientist, Center for Effective Organizations, May 2018.

238 Dana, J., Weber, R. A., & Kuang, J. X. (2007). Exploiting moral wiggle room: Experiments demonstrating an illusory preference for fairness. *Economic Theory,* 33(1), 67–80. doi:10.1007/s00199-006-0153-z

239 Feedback to the authors from Lucien Alziari, chief HR officer, CHRO Prudential, August 2018.

240 Ibid.

241 Effron, M. (2018). *8 steps to high performance.* Boston, MA: Harvard Business Press; Effron, M., & Ort, M. (2010). *One page talent management.* Boston, MA: Harvard Business Press.

242 Feedback to the authors from Kate Sweetman, founding principal, SweetmanCragun Group, July 2018.

243 Colquitt, A. L. (2017). *Next generation performance management.* Charlotte, NC: Information Age.

244 Churchill, W. (1941, February 09). Give Us The Tools. Retrieved November 5, 2018, from https://winstonchurchill.org/resources/speeches/1941-1945-war-leader/ give-us-the-tools/

245 Kuvaas, B., Buch, R., & Dysvik, A. (2017). Constructive supervisor feedback is not sufficient: Immediacy and frequency is essential. *Human Resource Management,* 56(3), 519–531. doi:10.1002/hrm.21785

246 Chhokar, J. S., & Wallin, J. A. (1984). A field study of the effect of feedback frequency on performance. *Journal of Applied Psychology,* 69(3), 524–530. doi:10.1037/0021-9010.69.3.524

247 Lam, C. F., DeRue, D. S., Karam, E. P., & Hollenbeck, J. R. (2011). The impact of feedback frequency on learning and task performance: Challenging the 'more is better' assumption. *Organizational Behavior and Human Decision Processes,* 116(2), 217–228. doi:10.1016/j.obhdp.2011.05.002

248 Kuhnen, C. M., & Tymula, A. (2012). Feedback, self-esteem, and performance in organizations. *Management Science,* 58(1), 94–113. doi:10.1287/mnsc.1110.1379

249 Van der Rijt, J., Van de Wiel, M. W. J., Van den Bossche, P., Segers, M. S. R., & Gijselaers, W. H. (2012). Contextual antecedents of informal feedback in the workplace. *Human Resource Development Quarterly,* 23(2), 233–257. doi:10.0.3.234/ hrdq.21129

250 Ertac, S. (2011). Does self-relevance affect information processing? Experimental evidence on the response to performance and non-performance feedback. *Journal of Economic Behavior & Organization*, 80(3), 532–545. doi:10.1016/j.jebo.2011.05.012

251 Kahneman, D. (2011). *Thinking, fast and slow.* New York, NY: Farrar, Straus and Giroux, p. 128.

252 Pfeffer, J. (2015). *Leadership BS: Fixing workplaces and careers one truth at a time.* New York, NY: Harper Business, p. 24.

253 Quoted in Weber, L., & Cook, L. (2018, 20 August). Too many bosses means too little time. *Wall Street Journal*. Retrieved 20 October 2018 from https://www.wsj.com/articles/too-many-bosses-means-too-little-time-1534766400

254 Krasman, J. (2011). Taking feedback-seeking to the next 'level': Organizational structure and feedback-seeking behavior. *Journal of Managerial Issues*, 23(1), 9–30.

255 Feedback to the authors from BTS executives, March 2018.

256 Feedback to the authors from Elaine Pulakos, president, PDRI, August 2018.

257 Noon, M. (2018). Pointless diversity training: Unconscious bias, new racism and agency. *Work, Employment and Society*, 32(1), 198–209. doi:10.1177/0950017017719841

258 Van der Rijt, J., Van de Wiel, M. W. J., Van den Bossche, P., Segers, M. S. R., & Gijselaers, W. H. (2012). Contextual antecedents of informal feedback in the workplace. *Human Resource Development Quarterly*, 23(2), 233–257. doi:10.0.3.234/hrdq.21129

259 Harrison, S. H., & Dossinger, K. (2017). Pliable guidance: A multilevel model of curiosity, feedback seeking, and feedback giving in creative work. *Academy of Management Journal*, 60(6), 2051–2072. doi:10.5465/amj.2015.0247

260 Feedback to the authors from Ellen Maag, partner at Heidrick & Struggles, September 2018.

261 Welch, J. (2013, November 14). Jack Welch: 'Rank-and-Yank'? That's Not How It's Done. *The Wall Street Journal*. Retrieved November 5, 2018, from https://www.wsj.com/articles/8216rankandyank8217-that8217s-not-how-it8217s-done-1384473281

262 This research suggests that such change may take 6–12 months but is totally possible. London, M., & Smither, J. W. (2002). Feedback orientation, feedback culture, and the longitudinal performance management process. *Human Resource Management Review*, 12(1), 81–100. doi:10.1016/S1053-4822(01)00043-2

263 Ibarra, H. (2015). *Act like a leader, think like a leader.* Boston, MA: Harvard Business Review Press.

ABOUT THE
AUTHORS

Angela Lane and **Sergey Gorbatov** work and write
about the complex science of human performance, while
making it simple. Leveraging Fortune 500 experience
gained across four continents, they equip leaders with
practical tools for success.